P9-DDU-779

Phaedrus

Agora Editions

Editor: Thomas L. Pangle

Founding Editor: Allan Bloom

Bolotin, David. *Plato's Dialogue on Friendship: An Interpretation of the "Lysis," with a New Translation*

Kojève, Alexandre. *Introduction to the Reading of Hegel: Lectures on the "Phenomenology of Spirit."* Assembled by Raymond Queneau. Edited by Allan Bloom. Translated by James H. Nichols Jr.

Medieval Political Philosophy: A Sourcebook. Edited by Ralph Lerner and Muhsin Mahdi

Plato. *Gorgias.* Translated by James H. Nichols Jr.

Plato. *Phaedrus.* Translated by James H. Nichols Jr.

Plato. *Gorgias* and *Phaedrus.* Translated by James H. Nichols Jr.

The Roots of Political Philosophy: Ten Forgotten Socratic Dialogues. Edited by Thomas L. Pangle.

Rousseau, Jean-Jacques. *Politics and the Arts: Letter to M. D'Alembert on the Theatre.* Translated by Allan Bloom

PLATO
Phaedrus

TRANSLATED WITH
INTRODUCTION, NOTES, AND AN
INTERPRETATIVE ESSAY BY

JAMES H. NICHOLS JR.

Cornell University Press

ITHACA AND LONDON

Copyright © 1998 by Cornell University

All rights reserved. Except for brief quotations in a review, this book, or parts
thereof, must not be reproduced in any form without permission in writing from
the publisher. For information, address Cornell University Press,
Sage House, 512 East State Street, Ithaca, New York 14850.

First published 1998 by Cornell University Press
First printing, Cornell Paperbacks, 1998

Printed in the United States of America

Library of Congress Cataloging-in-Publication Data

Plato
    [Phaedrus. English]
    Phaedrus / Plato ; translated with introduction, notes, and an
    interpretive essay by James H. Nichols, Jr.
        p.   cm.—(Agora paperback editions)
    Includes bibliographical references and index.
    ISBN 0-8014-8532-0 (pbk. : alk. paper).
    1. Love. 2. Rhetoric, Ancient. I. Nichols, James H., 1944– .
    II. Title. III. Series.
    B380.A5N53   1998
    184–dc21   98-27372

Cornell University Press strives to use environmentally responsible suppliers and
materials to the fullest extent possible in the publishing of its books. Such materials
include vegetable-based, low-VOC inks and acid-free papers that are recycled,
totally chlorine-free, or partly composed of nonwood fibers. Books that bear the
logo of the FSC (Forest Stewardship Council) use paper taken from forests that
have been inspected and certified as meeting the highest standards for environ-
mental and social responsibility. For further information, visit our website at
www.cornellpress.cornell.edu.

Paperback printing   10 9 8 7 6 5 4 3

Contents

Dialogue Names and Abbreviations

(Names appear spelled out at first instance and are abbreviated thereafter.)

Phaedrus

Socrates	SOC.
Phaedrus	PHAE.

Preface

The design and execution of this volume rest on three premises. First, that the questions regarding the nature of rhetoric and its proper relation to philosophy, politics, and education are of perennial concern and importance. Second, that Plato's investigation of these questions is profound and valuable for our own thinking. And third, that a careful translation by the same person of both *Gorgias* and *Phaedrus,* with notes and interpretative suggestions, could be very helpful for those wishing to come to grips with Plato's understanding of rhetoric.

Of course, I hold these premises to be true and to provide sufficient justification for the present volume. In fact, these premises seem to me sufficiently modest that I imagine most people might well agree with them. I further believe that substantially stronger assertions along each of these lines are defensible, though of necessity more controversial, and that these assertions make a far more compelling case for the value of this volume.

My full argument for these stronger assertions is to be found in the entirety of the volume that follows, including introduction, translations, notes, and suggestions for interpretation. Let me sketch them here briefly as follows.

First, rhetoric is the crucial link between philosophy and politics and must take an important place in education if political life and intellectual activity are to be in the best shape possible. While it is easy to denigrate the art of persuasion, most obviously by contrasting its possible deceptiveness with the truth of genuine knowledge, science, or philosophy, one should never forget the fundamental political fact that human beings must coordinate their activities with other human beings in order to live well, and

that the two most basic modes of such coordination are through persuasion and by force. Everyone knows the disadvantages of excessive reliance
by a political community on force or violence. If the highest intellectual
activities—science, philosophy—are to have much efficacy in practical political life, rhetoric must be the key intermediary.

Second, Plato presented the first full investigation of the most important
and fundamental questions about rhetoric, and its relation to philosophy
on the one hand and politics on the other. His investigation is classic, in the
sense that one can argue with plausibility that no later investigation has
surpassed its clarity and force on the basic questions. His understanding
of these questions and his philosophic suggestions about rhetoric deci-
sively affected the way these matters were viewed and dealt with for many
centuries and remain indispensable today.

Third, Plato's teaching on rhetoric is an aspect of his thought that is very
often misunderstood. Several features of the intellectual life of the last century or two make it difficult for many scholars to take the issue of rhetoric
as seriously as Plato himself did. Hence, for example, they are often mis-
led to think that, although the *Gorgias* does of course discuss rhetoric, it is
more deeply concerned with justice or philosophy. And similarly regarding the *Phaedrus*, many are reluctant to see rhetoric as its central theme.
New translations of both great Platonic dialogues on rhetoric, done by one
translator animated by the concern to recover a fuller and more adequate
understanding of Plato's teaching on rhetoric, may be just what the philosophical doctor ordered for those who sense the need to take a fresh and
sustained look at the problem of rhetoric.

So much for the overall design of this volume. Now a few words on particular aspects, starting with the translations. In his preface to *The Dialogues of Plato* (New Haven: Yale University Press, 1984), R. E. Allen makes
an elegant statement of a translator's need to make "the tactful adjustment
of competing demands which cannot each be fully satisfied" (xi–xii). He
discusses these demands under the names *fidelity, neutrality,* and *literalness.* My own adjustment puts considerable weight on literalness, with a
view to trying to provide the reader with as direct an access to Plato as possible and with as little dependency as possible on the translator's interpretative understanding. In the preface to *"The Republic" of Plato* (New
York: Basic Books, 1968), Allan Bloom's statement of the case against the
search for contemporaneous equivalents and in favor of a literalist tilting
of the balance is compelling—all the stronger, I find, because he criticizes
the leading nonliteral translations not by digging up some passages to

blame (which one can do to any translation) but by examining sample passages that the translators themselves singled out as exemplary of the excellence of their approach.

On the basis of my own experience, I would supplement Bloom's statement on behalf of literal translation in the following way. One could pursue the goal of being literal to whatever degree one might choose. But because words in two languages rarely correspond well in a one-to-one mapping, the more literal one wishes to be, the more notes one must add, either to explain one's word-for-word translation more fully, when necessary, so as not to mislead the reader; or where one cannot translate word for word, to point out that a particular Greek word is the same one that one has translated differently elsewhere. Too many such notes, however, would make the translation unbearable. One must therefore choose to which Greek words one will devote this close treatment and to which ones not. In the choice of where to be fully literal and to add notes, one cannot help subjecting the reader to dependence on one's interpretation.

That statement of the problem does not vitiate the goal of choosing to be literal rather than not, up to a point. It simply clarifies just why the goal of literalness can be attained only within some limits, and it suggests that the translator might well try to indicate what the principles of choice in that domain have been. The reader may of course gain fuller information on that point by looking at the actual notes to the translation itself.

Here I wish to indicate three principles by which my own choice of when to strive for literalness has been guided. First, as my opening remarks on rhetoric suggest, I pay especially close literal attention to words related to rhetoric, persuasion, speech, and the like. Second—a principle that, regrettably, I find myself able to state only vaguely—I strive for especial literalness with those words that most people concerned with philosophy, morality, and politics consider of obviously central importance (*the good, the beautiful, the just, the city, love, wisdom,* and so on). Third, any Greek expressions which, when translated literally, may sound odd but yet do not really mislead, I try to translate quite literally (oaths, terms for superhuman beings, strange vocatives, and the like).

The notes to the translation are chiefly philological and historical, rather than interpretative. I have just admitted, of course, that my philological notes explanatory to the translation rest implicitly, at least in part, on an overall interpretation; yet such notes are in themselves linguistic rather than interpretative, and I have expressed my interpretation in the introduction and in the essays on each dialogue. The historical notes aim to provide necessary or useful information, mostly noncontroversial, to facilitate understanding of the dialogues by readers who are not especially learned in ancient Greek literature or history. In addition to these two types of notes, I have pointed out certain parallels, references, or contrasts between the *Gorgias* and the *Phaedrus*.

Whole books have been written on each of these fascinating dialogues. My interpretative essays propose lines of interpretation concerning what I take to be the central theme of rhetoric. Given their brevity and the limitations of their author's own understanding, these essays are meant to be suggestive, not definitive, and I have no doubt that my readers will take them in that spirit.

In the introduction, I begin by reflecting on our present circumstances as regards rhetoric and how we got there. I introduce Plato's examination of rhetoric by arguing first that both dialogues do indeed have rhetoric as their central theme. I seek to set the stage for the more detailed study of these dialogues by presenting some preliminary thoughts on why Plato gave us two dialogues on this theme and on how these two dialogues relate to each other.

My translation of the *Phaedrus* is based on J. Burnet, *Platonis Opera*, Oxford Classical Texts, vol. 2 (Oxford: Clarendon Press, 1901). I have repeatedly consulted the learned notes presented by G. J. De Vries (and have often followed his readings where different from Burnet's) in his *Commentary on the "Phaedrus" of Plato* (Amsterdam: A. M. Hakkert, 1969), and in my own notes all references to De Vries are to that commentary. I have throughout also consulted the translation and notes of Léon Robin, *Platon: Oeuvres Complètes* (Greek text and French translation), Tome IV—3ᵉ Partie: *Phèdre* (Paris: Société d'Edition Les Belles Lettres, 1954).

My companion translation of the *Gorgias* is based on the edition of E. R. Dodds, *Plato; Gorgias* (A Revised Text with Introduction and Commentary) (Oxford: Clarendon Press, 1959). I have constantly relied on his learned notes, and in my own notes all references to Dodds are to his commentary on the Greek text. Throughout I have also consulted the detailed and careful philosophical analyses of the *Gorgias* presented by Terence Irwin, *Plato; Gorgias* (Translated with Notes) (Oxford: Clarendon Press, 1979). In the fall of 1976, while I was teaching a seminar on the *Gorgias* (at the Graduate Faculty of the New School), I read the transcript (since mislaid) of a seminar given on the dialogue by Leo Strauss at the University of Chicago; I want to acknowledge my intellectual debt to that most thought-provoking seminar.

I have frequently used the great dictionary (abbreviated in my notes as LSJ) *A Greek-English Lexicon,* by H. G. Liddell and R. S. Scott, new edition revised and augmented by H. S. Jones (Oxford: Clarendon Press, 1940 [reprinted 1961]).

I wish to acknowledge the generous assistance provided me by the Lynde and Harry Bradley Foundation, for which I am most grateful. Thanks to this assistance I was able to extend a sabbatical and take some additional leave to work on this lengthy project. I have also benefited from the sabbatical granted me by Claremont McKenna College and by a summer grant from Claremont McKenna College's Gould Center for the Humanities.

During the twenty years in which I worked with varying degrees of intensity on these dialogues of Plato, I received intellectual support, criticism, and suggestions from many friends and colleagues and benefited from much conversation with them as well as with students. Among those to whom I am grateful for discussions about Plato on many occasions are Victor Baras, Allan Bloom, David Bolotin, Christopher Bruell, Hillel Fradkin, Arthur Melzer, and Thomas Pangle. I want to acknowledge valuable comments on various parts of this work, comments that I have received from Joseph Bessette, James Ceaser, Lorraine Smith Pangle, and Paul Ulrich, and to thank Cornell University Press's anonymous reader for unusually thorough, careful, and helpful suggestions.

Without the encouragement of my wife, Merle Naomi Stern, I doubt that I should ever have completed this work. I dedicate it to her.

Phaedrus

Introduction: Rhetoric, Philosophy, and Politics

In less than a century and a half, our public discourse has undergone an astonishing decline. The remarkable eloquence of leading public speakers from an earlier time finds hardly a weak echo in the present. This difference may be explained, at least in part, by the difference in political situation. Then, the greatest political issues were at stake, strife verging on civil war tore the republic apart, and political rhetoric rose to meet these challenges. Now, we enjoy stable political tranquillity, and our public speech, concerned with smaller matters, has sunk to a lower level.

So say participants in Tacitus's *Dialogue on Oratory*, who compare the public speakers of their own time with Cicero.[1] Would we not take a similar view if we should set speeches by leading political figures today next to those of Abraham Lincoln?

Now, although some speakers in Tacitus refer the decline of rhetoric to the blessings of political stability in their time, we may be sure that this cheerful thought is not the whole story for Tacitus. All his works are meditations on the causes and consequences of the loss of republican self-government. He makes it abundantly clear that his time differs from Rome's glorious past most importantly in its being ruled no longer in a republican but in a basically monarchical and sometimes tyrannical manner. That change has profound effects on political speech.

---

1. Tacitus, *Dialogue on Oratory*, sections 24 and 36. Cicero is referred to as active about 120 years before the dialogue's dramatic date.

1

Likewise today, no sensible observer could attribute the decline in our political rhetoric solely to the absence of imminent danger of civil war. We seem, to be sure, nowhere near the loss of republican government; yet we can nonetheless detect signs of substantially decreased public participation in politics, less sustained attention to and less clear understanding of political affairs, less widespread experience in political speech. Has some formerly available knowledge about rhetoric and politics slipped from our habitual grasp? Surely the reasons one might give for a decline in our political speech are all too multifarious. Perhaps everyone's favorite culprit is the rise of mass media, which appear to bring ever-shortening attention spans to the ever less thoughtful minds of the mass political audience. Each of the Lincoln-Douglas debates lasted three hours: an opening speech of one hour, followed by the second speaker's address lasting an hour and a half, and concluded with a half hour's rebuttal by the first. Our televised presidential debates are short responses to journalists' questions; and the length of the average excerpt from a presidential candidate's speech presented on national network news broadcasts in a recent election was seventeen seconds.

Crucial to the degradation of our political speech, I believe, are confusion about what rhetoric is and inattention to its necessary and proper place in politics and in education. These failures of understanding have contributed to a decline in the study and thoughtful practice of rhetoric.

Today's lack of clarity about rhetoric can be seen most evidently in the confusingly varied ways in which we use the term *rhetoric*. Rhetoric's precise nature and scope remain altogether indeterminate. In particular, popular usage and the most advanced academic usage of the term diverge sharply. *Rhetoric* in popular usage is almost always a term of disparagement. The phrase "mere rhetoric" typically designates deceptively fashioned speech whose meaning stands at odds with the speaker's real purposes. Politicians are taunted by their opponents and exhorted by political commentators to cut out the rhetoric and tell us what they would really do to deal with our problems. Many intellectuals reflect this point of view when, in treating some topic or other, they set *rhetoric* and *reality* in opposition to each other. A completely different usage occurs, however, among academics influenced by the latest academic trend, postmodernism. Such academics tend to give an immensely broad meaning to *rhetoric*: it is the study and practice of how discourse is carried on in any area whatsoever, comprehending the rules of discourse that obtain in any area as well as an account of how they came into being and continue to change. In accordance with this usage, we would have rhetorics pertaining to the whole range of subject matters from literary criticism to economics and even mathematics.[2]

In the time of Socrates, too, *rhetoric* was a much-disputed term, as we see most clearly in Plato's dialogues. Gorgias in the dialogue named for him believes that his art or science of rhetoric is the greatest of human goods and the cause of freedom for oneself and rule over others. By contrast, Socrates declares his view that what is generally called rhetoric is no art at all, but the mere knack of a certain kind of flattery. Socrates distinguishes rhetoric from sophistry but indicates that they are often confused with each other. Later in the dialogue, however, Socrates suggests the possibility of a real art of rhetoric that would serve justice and the political good. When Socrates questions Gorgias in search of just what Gorgias's rhetoric is, Socrates narrows down the definition to public persuasion of large groups and distinguishes mere persuasion of that sort from teaching the truth about things. Speaking for himself in the *Phaedrus*, by contrast, Socrates suggests a broad definition of rhetoric that would apply to individuals as well as groups and would include the teaching of genuine knowledge. What, then, is rhetoric for Plato's Socrates?

If it is correct that our own time experiences considerable confusion about what rhetoric is, we might receive especially valuable help in clarifying our thinking by studying Plato's treatment of this matter. Plato confronted a similarly complex situation, and the understanding he elaborated set the terms for reflection on rhetoric for a long time to come. The present volume seeks to facilitate rethinking of the problem of rhetoric through new translations, together with suggestions for interpretation, of Plato's two great dialogues on rhetoric.

Rhetoric Then and Now

Socrates tells Phaedrus that a speech about something on which people hold differing opinions should begin with a definition. Rhetoric certainly appears to be such a subject, both now and at times in the past. It is hard to know which of the many competing definitions to choose as a basis for further discussion.

2. An impressive example of this approach is Donald McCloskey's *The Rhetoric of Economics* (Madison: University of Wisconsin Press, 1985).

Rhetoric clearly has to do with speaking well. But because people spoke well or poorly before anyone talked about an art of rhetoric, doubtless we should reserve the term *rhetoric* for a skill, art, or science of speaking well that has consciously and explicitly reflected on what makes for good and bad speaking. Within the Western tradition, such conscious reflection about speech emerged among the Greek Sophists, most notably Gorgias and Protagoras. It is not altogether clear how they conceived of their rhetorical art, for instance whether they clearly distinguished it from sophistry as a whole; in this respect their use of the term may well have something in common with the expansive postmodernist usage that I have already referred to. Indeed, postmodernists often praise sophistic rhetoric and deplore its loss of respectability from Plato's vigorous attack on it.

In the aftermath of Plato's effective critique of sophistic rhetoric and his suggestions for a philosophically guided rhetoric, however, rhetoric came to be conceived of in a way that remained stable in its essentials for most of Western history, and it is this conception of rhetoric that I wish to deal with now. Let me begin to sketch what rhetoric thus conceived is by presenting two definitions of it, definitions separated by nearly two millennia. Aristotle calls it "the power [or capacity or ability] in each [case whatsoever] of discerning the available means of persuasion."[3] By also calling rhetoric the counterpart of dialectic, Aristotle makes its scope in one way very broad; but its chief persuasive applications lead it to deal mainly with the kinds of matters dealt with by the sciences of politics and ethics. Francis Bacon speaks of rhetoric or the art of eloquence this way in the *Advancement of Learning:* "a science excellent, and excellently well laboured. For although in true value it is inferior to wisdom, as it is said by God to Moses, . . . it is eloquence that prevaileth in an active life. . . . The duty and office of rhetoric is to apply reason to imagination for the better moving of the will."[4]

However much these two definitions may differ, their agreement appears more substantial and important than their differences. Both distinguish between the substance of what one wishes to persuade (or the direction in which one wishes to move the will) and the verbal means of effecting that persuasion (or of actually moving the will). For both, rhetoric is very important in human life, especially, of course, in practical and, above all, political affairs. Without rhetorical capacity, the wise man or

---

3. Aristotle, *Rhetoric* 1355b. An accurate and helpfully annotated new translation is Aristotle, *On Rhetoric: A Theory of Civic Discourse,* trans. George A. Kennedy (New York: Oxford University Press, 1991).
4. Francis Bacon, *Advancement of Learning* 2.18.1–2.

man of knowledge can have no important effect in politics or in other human activities. Though its importance is great, rhetoric is lower in rank than science or wisdom itself. Rhetoric is not the whole of knowledge, nor even the whole of political skill and wisdom, as some Sophists may well have believed; yet it is neither negligible nor something whose importance one might reasonably foresee diminishing with time.

Rhetoric thus understood had an important place in higher education for centuries, one might say from the time of Aristotle to 1800 or so.[5] The rhetoric of the Greeks was learned and further developed by Roman orators and authors, most notably Cicero and Quintilian. In the medieval trivium of grammar, rhetoric, and logic, rhetoric's place was secure. Its scope was diminished in some respects, notably its primary use in political affairs, but expanded in others, for instance in the development of *ars praedictionis,* the rhetorical art of preaching sermons.[6] The recovery of the wisdom of antiquity by Renaissance humanism gave renewed dignity to rhetoric, in particular by reviving its civic function, which had been crucial for Aristotle and for ancient republicanism generally. Accordingly, Cicero was arguably the preeminent figure from classical antiquity for the writers and thinkers of the early Renaissance. With much variation in approach, basis, and emphasis, rhetoric remained important well into the eighteenth and nineteenth centuries: Adam Smith, for instance, gave lectures on rhetoric and belles lettres in addition to his better-known teachings on moral philosophy, jurisprudence, and political economy.[7]

Why then did rhetoric subsequently fall into eclipse? One cause was a certain way of thinking about Enlightenment. Although Francis Bacon, among the greatest founders of the Enlightenment movement, held a high view of the importance of rhetoric, Thomas Hobbes in the very next generation took a dim view of it, and John Locke a still dimmer one soon after. Hear John Locke:

> If we would speak of Things as they are, we must allow, that all the Art of Rhetorick, besides Order and Clearness, all the artificial and figurative ap-

5. So Thomas Cole puts it in his *Origins of Rhetoric in Ancient Greece* (Baltimore: Johns Hopkins University Press, 1991), p. 22.

6. On rhetoric in the Middle Ages, Murphy's introduction is helpful, in James J. Murphy, ed. *Three Medieval Rhetorical Arts* (Berkeley: University of California Press, 1971).

7. A good overall history is George A. Kennedy, *Classical Rhetoric and Its Christian and Secular Tradition from Ancient to Modern Times* (Chapel Hill: University of North Carolina Press, 1980).

plication of Words Eloquence hath invented, are for nothing else but to in-
sinuate wrong *Ideas*, move the Passions, and thereby mislead the Judgment; and so indeed are perfect cheat. . . . 'Tis evident how much Men love
to deceive, and be deceived, since Rhetorick, that powerful instrument of
Error and Deceit, has its established Professors, is publickly taught, and has
always been had in great Reputation.[8]

Rhetoric's power of deception has been an issue from the start, but it
looks especially questionable from an Enlightenment point of view. Let me
put the central idea of Enlightenment this way: the progress of knowledge,
philosophy, and science naturally harmonizes, in the long run, with the
overall well-being of political community as a whole. Most of us to this
day remain heirs of the Enlightenment to such an extent that we are inclined to accept that idea without much ado, but it bears emphasizing that
it is a relatively new view. Plato, for instance, did not share it. His most famous image of political society is the cave, whose members live not in the
light of the truth but with shared perceptions of shadows of man-made
artifacts.[9] The good functioning of society depends on consensus, shared
judgments, common sentiments, and the like. Philosophy disrupts all these,
of necessity, through its critical testing of mere opinion in search for genuine truths. Does the philosopher attain the truth he seeks? One cannot
confidently answer yes; Socrates, who appears in Plato's writings as the
very model of the seeker after truth, never claims to possess wisdom or
knowledge about the most important matters. If a philosopher did attain
the comprehensive or highest truth—or even truth about many of the most
important things—could truth be directly applied to make society simply
rational, or even just to improve it overall? The answer to this question is
no less uncertain. Given these two levels of uncertainties, it seems reasonable to suppose that a philosopher would always need rhetoric if he is to
be able to have any beneficial political effect at all; indeed he would need
rhetoric even for the mere presentation of his philosophical views in a politically responsible and defensible manner.

By contrast, in an Enlightenment perspective, our hopes are oriented toward the spread of real and solid knowledge. Rhetoric may be needed
now, but it should become less necessary the more progress we make. Jefferson, himself a gifted rhetorician, expresses these Enlightenment hopes

8. John Locke, *An Essay concerning Human Understanding*, bk. 3, chap. 10, sec. 34.
9. Plato, *The Republic* 7.514a–521c.

in 1826, when he writes of the fateful decision and declaration of a half-century before:

> May it be to the world, what I believe it will be (to some parts sooner, to others later, but finally to all), the signal of arousing men to burst the chains under which monkish ignorance and superstition had persuaded them to bind themselves, and to assume the blessings and security of self-government. . . . All eyes are opened, or opening, to the rights of man. The general spread of the light of science has already laid open to every view the palpable truth, that the mass of mankind has not been born with saddles on their backs, nor a favored few booted and spurred, ready to ride them legitimately, by the grace of God. These are grounds of hope for others.[10]

With the bright light of science thus ever more broadly diffused, what need for rhetoric? Surely, one seems justified to hope, a diminishing one. In the long run, the deceitful appeals and devious wiles of rhetoric will be more obstacle than help in the course of human progress.

A second, later intellectual force that drove rhetoric from its former place in education and intellectual life was the Romantic conception of Art. Indeed, this strand of thinking is more deeply opposed to the traditional conception and place of rhetoric than the Enlightenment view, and we remain, I believe, at least as much under its sway as under the other's. This conception of Art, emerging in critical reaction to certain features of the Enlightenment's worldview, holds that the highest achievements of the human spirit are the creative productions of the unique individual.[11]

---

10. Thomas Jefferson, *Selected Writings,* ed. Harvey C. Mansfield Jr. (Arlington Heights, Ill.: AHM Publishing, 1979), p. 12.

11. Let me cite three scholars who state this basic view from widely different perspectives. Brian Vickers, speaking of why it is hard for us to grasp rhetoric's past importance, states that "a prolonged effort of the historical imagination is necessary. We have to overcome . . . the distrust and opposition to rhetoric that have prevailed in European poetics and aesthetics since the post-Romantic generation" (Brian Vickers, ed., *Rhetoric Revalued: Papers from the International Society for the History of Rhetoric,* [Binghampton, N.Y.: Center for Medieval & Renaissance Studies, 1982], p. 13). Leo Strauss, speaking of the eclipse in the reputations of Xenophon, Livy, and Cicero, writes that it "has been due to a decline in the understanding of the significance of rhetoric: both the peculiar 'idealism' and the peculiar 'realism' of the 19th century were guided by the modern conception of 'Art' and for that reason were unable to understand the crucial significance of the lowly art of rhetoric" (Leo Strauss, *On Tyranny,* [New York: Free Press, 1963], p. 26). Thomas Cole refers to the "decline of the discipline in the past two centuries," which he connects to "the widely held romantic or 'expressionist' notion of the literary work as a unique or maximally adequate verbalization of a unique vision or unique individual sensibility" (*Origins of Rhetoric,* p. 19).

Let me elaborate on the ground and character of this notion by considering how it might originate from an aspect of Rousseau's thought. He makes clear that the real world as illuminated by Enlightenment philosophy and modern science has nothing in it that can satisfy our specifically human needs, concerns, passions. The human being itself, as merely natural, is subhuman, without speech, reason, society, and the arts. The natural world, as matter in motion, has no inherent beauty or appeal to our full humanity: "The existence of finite beings is so poor and so limited that when we only see what is, we are never moved. It is chimeras that adorn real objects, and if the imagination does not add a charm to what strikes us, the sterile pleasure that one takes in it is limited to the organ and always leaves the heart cold."[12] Beauty is created for us by our imagination, cultivated and developed as we move away from nature. So too, that most powerful and distinctively human passion of love is "chimera, lie, illusion. One loves much more the image that one makes for oneself than the object to which one applies it. If one saw what one loves exactly as it is, there would be no more love on earth."[13] The greatest human achievements are those of the unique genius—poet, artist, musician, and (possibly) prophet or lawgiver—whose greatness is measured by the integrity of vision and its capacity to enrich the lives of others, even whole peoples or civilizations. Only through being molded by the formative influence on their imaginations of such unique visions can people come to participate in full humanity. Not knowledge of nature, nor art as imitation of nature, but artistic creation represents the peak of humanity.

From this point of view regarding what is of the highest human worth, rhetoric is lowly indeed. Its consciously manipulative aspect is not just something different from artistic creation, but flagrantly contradicts the whole spirit of attaining and expressing one's individual vision. The self-conscious and calculated working out of the best way persuasively to state one's purpose stands diametrically opposed to authentic artistic creativity. As Keats said, "Poetry should come as naturally as the leaves to a tree: otherwise it had better not come at all."[14] Rousseau himself does not take this view; like Bacon, he greatly appreciates the classic tradition of rhetoric. But later modern trends, in losing the close touch that Rousseau still main-

---

12. Rousseau, *Oeuvres Complètes*, ed. Bernard Gagnebin and Marcel Raymond (Paris: Gallimard, Bibliothèque de la Pléiade, 1959–1969), 4:418.
13. Rousseau, *Oeuvres Complètes*, 4:656.
14. Keats, letter to John Taylor, 27 February 1818, cited by Ian Thomson, "Rhetoric and the Passions, 1760–1800," in Vickers, ed., *Rhetoric Revalued*, p. 146.

tained with classical thought and its deeply political concerns, develop this modern notion of Art in a way that leaves rhetoric as something quite contemptible: manipulative, basely calculating, falsely separating form from content, concerned with low utility, and of course deceptive.

As if the Enlightenment view of the progressive diffusion of knowledge and the Romantic view of Art were not enemies enough for the older tradition of rhetoric, democratic egalitarianism directs yet another objection to it, an old one with a new wrinkle. Although rhetoric seems naturally to flourish best in republics, democracy nonetheless has a certain hostility toward it. Because democracy rests on a kind of assumption that all are equal in the most important political respect, why should rhetoric be needed? It does not appear to be a specialized expertise, like medicine, to which it is sensible for all nonexperts to defer. If it does accomplish something, does it not thereby disrupt democratic equality, by helping the few, those with sufficient leisure and money to study rhetoric, to prevail over the many?

This problem of rhetoric's elitism, like the issue of deception, has been around from the start. Plato deals with it as we shall see in the *Gorgias* and delicately touches on it in the *Protagoras*, where Socrates compels that famous Sophist to come to terms with the problematic relation of sophistry to democracy. The problem perseveres in modern democracy, reinforced by a relativism about good and bad, noble and base things, which Plato himself had already diagnosed as an endemic tendency of democratic thinking and character. The democratic man, Socrates argues, "doesn't admit true speech . . . , if someone says that there are some pleasures belonging to fine and good desires and some belonging to bad desires, and that the ones must be practiced and honored and the others checked and enslaved. Rather, he shakes his head at all this and says that all are alike and must be honored on an equal basis."[15] The peculiar feature of our situation is that that view, in several more elaborated versions, has come to prevail in the most advanced intellectual circles. Consequently, the traditional defense of rhetoric as necessary to link wisdom to the level of understanding of the many tends to be angrily or derisively rejected as elitist, without a serious hearing. Our late modern or postmodernist sophistication is supposed to have taught us that no sweeping claims of superior knowledge regarding values can be accepted, or even examined seriously.

And yet today the discussion of rhetoric is going on full tilt, to such a degree that one can properly speak of a sharp revival of interest in rhetoric.

15. Plato, *Republic* 8.561b–c.

The most easily available evidence of this trend can be discovered through inspecting the growing number of book titles that mention rhetoric. Scholarly articles that analyze rhetoric or rhetorical aspects in literature, philosophy, and political theory likewise abound. How can this be? The key to understanding this development, I believe, is to be found in the hugely expanded sense of the term *rhetoric* that has emerged under the influence of postmodernism. Along lines drawn by Nietzsche and plowed more deeply by Heidegger, postmodernism continues the project of uprooting the Western philosophical tradition. That tradition's search for metaphysical foundations; its impulse toward what is permanent and universal rather than transient and local; its dichotomies of belief and knowledge, subject and object, truth and opinion, appearance and reality, science and rhetoric—all these ways of thinking, it is asserted, have proven to be dead ends, habits that our riper experience and reflection should lead us to outgrow. Mode of presentation, therefore, cannot be tenably distinguished from the substance of what is intended; form cannot be separated usefully from content; rhetoric cannot be soundly differentiated from science or philosophy or political goal. All discourse is rhetorical.

Now, this new way of talking about rhetoric is surely thought-provoking, doubtless contains elements of truth, and, in my judgment, may have the intellectually salutary effect of discrediting overly narrow methodologies, especially in the social sciences.[16] Yet I must wonder whether a term used so broadly as *rhetoric* is now used does not lose its usefulness for clarifying our thinking. I must wonder, too, whether we do not still need to make the distinctions that used to be made with the former meaning of the term *rhetoric*. Let us grant that many dichotomies can be misleading or narrowing if taken in a rigid or dogmatic manner. But must one not worry on the other side about unintended effects that may emerge if we reject useful, commonsensical, perhaps indispensable distinctions in our thinking? However much we may need critically to call into question the adequacy of our understanding of, say, our desire to discover permanent truths, is our thought really deepened or, on the contrary, is it rendered more superficial by dismissing such terms as obsolete relics of exploded metaphysics? After all, did not human beings display concern for truth as distinguished from hearsay or falsehood long before Plato or anyone else laid down the supposedly metaphysical foundations of Western thinking?

Postmodernist approaches in philosophy and politics seem to me at their most useful in bringing to light and criticizing distinctive features of

16. McCloskey's work in economics seems especially valuable in this regard; see note 2.

various leading traditions of modern thought (taking *modern* to mean dating from Bacon or Descartes or thereabouts). But similar critiques addressed to ancient thought appear to me far less revealing, because they seem often to rest for the most part on simplistic readings of ancient authors. This defect is most glaring as regards Plato. The eagerness to reject his allegedly rigid or absolutist dichotomies leads critics often to take tentative suggestions in Platonic dialogues for declared and settled doctrine; to ignore the significance of the context in which speakers make assertions in the dialogues; to pass over the professions of uncertainty with which assertions are framed (or to note them dismissively as mere Socratic window dressing used by the dogmatic Plato).

In fine, the postmodernist style of rejecting allegedly Platonic doctrines typically rests on simplistic accounts of what Plato is supposed to have held; especially so as regards rhetoric. Cicero's Crassus says that, in carefully reading the *Gorgias,* he admired Plato most in that "he himself seemed to me to be the supreme orator in ridiculing the orators."[17] Should not this intelligent observation motivate us to interpret Plato's critique of rhetoric with some nuance, subtlety, and irony? But instead, all too often we find Plato described simply as the bitter enemy of rhetoric.[18]

But if rhetoric should be as important as I have suggested, or as many writers today seem to think, or as most of the Western intellectual tradition appears to have held, surely it is worthwhile to look closely, with sympathetic attention, at how Plato investigated the problem of rhetoric in relation to philosophy and politics.

PRELIMINARY SKETCH OF RHETORIC'S IMPORTANCE FOR PLATO:
The Apology of Socrates AND *The Republic*

For rhetoric, as for many another important theme in Plato, *The Apology of Socrates* provides a most helpful beginning point for reflection. The *Apology* or defense speech begins with Socrates' statements on the problem of rhetoric. People skilled in rhetoric are often described as terribly clever at speaking, and Socrates' accusers have so characterized him in their speech

17. Cicero, *De Oratore* 1.47
18. For instance: Brian Vickers, *In Defence of Rhetoric* (Oxford: Clarendon Press, 1988). This book provides a valuable discussion and defense of rhetoric throughout history; but its interpretation of Plato's views of rhetoric is its weakest spot, wherein Vickers lets himself go into indignant exclamations about Plato's unfairness to Gorgias. George Kennedy's mostly excellent *Art of Persuasion in Ancient Greece* (Princeton: Princeton University Press, 1963), p. 14, likewise refers too simply to Gorgias as "the butt of [Plato's] invective against rhetoric."

before the Athenian judicial body of some five hundred citizens. Socrates denies this charge; indeed he describes it as his accusers' most shameless accusation, because they will be immediately refuted in deed by Socrates' own defense speech. But as with so many Socratic statements, this one has its complexities. Not only does this beginning of his speech exemplify some sound rhetorical technique (aiming at presenting one's character in such a way as to dispose one's hearers favorably), but Socrates himself qualifies his own disclaimer, at least hypothetically: if the accusers call terribly clever him who says true things, then Socrates agrees that he is a rhetor, though not after their manner.[19]

Socrates denies that he uses the sort of verbal devices that are usually thought to constitute rhetorically artful speech. Instead, he urges the five hundred judges to overlook his manner of speaking and to consider only whether he says just things or not; for this, he asserts, is the virtue of a judge; the virtue of a rhetor is to say true things. Thus, in his only address to the political multitude of Athens of which we have record, Socrates starts with a reflection on rhetoric and truth and emphatically draws attention to his unusual, almost foreign, views on these matters.[20]

Several times in the course of his defense speech, Socrates comments on what makes persuasion difficult in his circumstances. Despite his facing a capital charge, he must deal in but a short time with deeply rooted, because ancient, slanders. The character of Athenian political and especially judicial practices leads the jurors to expect improper things from a defendant. Socrates offers what is perhaps his most revealing comment on persuading the jurors when he has been found guilty and must propose an alternative punishment to the death sentence demanded by the prosecution. He reflects on how difficult it is to persuade them that he must carry on his present way of life unchanged. If he says that to do otherwise would be to disobey the god, "you will not be persuaded by me, on the grounds that I am being ironical." But if he asserts that his philosophic life is the greatest good for a human being and that the unexamined life is not worth living, "you will be even less persuaded by me as I say these things. But they are so, as I assert, men, but it is not easy to persuade."[21]

19. Plato, *The Apology of Socrates* 17b.
20. Plato, *Apology* 17d–18a. We know from *Apology* 32a–c that Socrates spoke to the democratic assembly in support of the lawful way of proceeding in the matter of the admirals after the battle of Arginusae; Socrates' arguments did not, however, prevail over the rhetors on that occasion either.
21. Plato, *Apology* 38a.

The *Apology* dramatizes unforgettably the most urgent, and perhaps the central, problem of political philosophy: the tension between the philosopher and the city. Socrates fails at political persuasion; the truth is politically inefficacious and unacceptable.[22] The *Apology* displays in deed what Socrates predicts in the *Gorgias* (521c–522c): that his dialectical mode of speaking with one person at a time cannot work with the many; that if accused before a multitude, he would be left gaping, with nothing to say. He would be like a doctor, administrator of surgery, cautery, bitter drugs, and harsh diets, accused by a pastry chef before a jury of children. Yet we see in the *Apology* that Socrates was willing to make *some* effort to persuade the judges: in his main defense speech he did, after all, present the more popularly persuasive account of his life as a divine mission; he did not simply develop arguments to show how his way of life is in truth the greatest human good. And he plainly asserts to those who condemned him to death that he could have found the arguments by which to get himself acquitted. What caused his condemnation was not being at a loss for speeches. It was his unwillingness to say and to do all things (including shameful things), his judgment that one ought not use all devices to avoid death, in battle or in courtroom, that led to his condemnation.[23]

If we held political rhetoric to be the capacity to persuade a political multitude to acquit one of a charge, we should have to say that Socrates possessed that rhetorical capacity but chose not to use it. Socrates is not quite the foreigner to political rhetoric that he seemed at first.

If the *Republic* is the true *apologia* of Socrates before the city,[24] one would expect to find there too some crucial reflections on rhetoric, philosophy, and politics; and the *Republic* does not disappoint in this regard. For one thing, the overall direction of discussion is set by the rhetorician Thrasymachus's contribution. It is his debunking of justice as mere convention and his praise of successful injustice that provoke Socrates to a prolonged defense of justice; thus we see the familiar and conventional picture of Socrates fighting against the rhetoricians or the sophists. And yet, at about midpoint in the discussion, Socrates asserts that he and Thrasymachus

---

22. Thinkers of the Enlightenment sought to overcome this tension by making truth politically efficacious and by reforming political society in accordance with reason's prescriptions. By now, however, most political scientists recognize that that hopeful endeavor has met with but partial success, at most.

23. Plato, *Apology* 38d–39a.

24. As Allan Bloom has argued persuasively in *"The Republic" of Plato* (New York: Basic Books, 1968), p. 307.

"have just become friends, though we weren't even enemies before."[25] How are we to understand this remarkable utterance? Its significance, I believe, lies in the context: Socrates' account of the philosopher rulers has made clear the crucial need for persuasion if the best city is to become a reality. He has recently exhorted Adeimantus to "teach the image [of the philosopher on the ship of the city] to that man who wonders at the philosophers' not being honored in the cities, and try to *persuade* him that it would be far more to be wondered at if they were honored."[26] He has exonerated private sophists from blame for corrupting young men, asserting instead that not any private person but the political multitude is the biggest sophist.[27] And he is about to temper Adeimantus's contempt (perhaps mixed with fear) of the opinions of the many by saying to him: "Don't make such a severe accusation against the many. They will no doubt have another sort of opinion, if instead of indulging yourself in quarreling with them, you soothe them and do away with the slander against the love of learning by pointing out whom you mean by the philosophers. . . ."[28] In the *Phaedrus* (267c–d) Socrates refers to Thrasymachus's special capacity to arouse or soothe angry passion and to slander or to dissipate slanders: within this context of the *Republic*, then, Socrates is sketching a crucial task that calls for the capacities precisely of Thrasymachus. Socrates concludes this segment of discussion by speaking as follows of those who his interlocutor had supposed would be angry at the notion that philosophers should rule: "'If you please,' I said, 'let's not say that they are less angry but that they have become in every way gentle and have been persuaded, so that from shame, if nothing else, they will agree.' 'Most certainly,' he said. 'Now, let's assume they have been persuaded of this,' I said."[29]

At this point in the *Republic*, then, Socrates appears to attribute very great power to the capacity to persuade. But is this the whole story, and his final judgment, on the power of rhetoric? To the contrary, one must remember the crucial introductory scene of the dialogue, which provided an urbane, comical representation of the twofold character of politics as consisting of both persuasion and force. To Polemarchus's proposition that Socrates and Glaucon must either prove stronger than his group or else

25. Plato, *Republic* 6.498c–d. This friendship does not prevent Socrates from once again making clear that Thrasymachus praises injustice and hence tyranny (8.545a).
26. Plato, *Republic* 6.489a, emphasis added.
27. Plato, *Republic* 6.492a–b.
28. Plato, *Republic* 6.499e.
29. Plato, *Republic* 6.501e–502a.

stay in the Piraeus, Socrates suggested the alternative possibility of "our persuading you that you must let us go." But, Polemarchus asked, "Could you really persuade, if we don't listen?"[30] Surely Plato thus reminds us of the ever-present limitations on the power of rhetoric. Accordingly, although education in the *Republic* as a whole does indeed use rhetorical persuasion, it also works through habituation from a very early age, laws with penalties, and even deceptive uses of authoritative divine ceremonies like sacred lotteries. Rhetoric may be powerful but it is surely not all-powerful.

Rhetoric as the Central Theme of the *Gorgias* and *Phaedrus*

Just how powerful is rhetoric? That is the question in Socrates' mind when he goes with his friend Chaerephon to the place where the famous rhetorician Gorgias has been displaying his art. In explaining his desire to converse with Gorgias, Socrates tells Callicles that he wants to learn "what the power of the man's art is, and what it is that he professes and teaches" (447c).

The interlocutors in the *Gorgias* deal with the most important questions— such great matters as whether justice or injustice is superior, and whether the philosophic life or the life of political action is best for a human being. What is more, Socrates speaks about these things with a degree of passionate engagement that many a reader finds deeply moving. For these reasons, many commentators reject the view that the dialogue is chiefly about rhetoric. They prefer to take the investigation of rhetoric as merely the occasion for a discussion that moves on to weightier philosophic and moral questions.[31] Without in any way denying that loftier subjects are indeed discussed in the dialogue at considerable length, I nonetheless wish to maintain that what ties the dialogue into a whole and makes sense of its several parts is indeed what Socrates had in mind from the start, namely the question of rhetoric and its power. In this place I shall briefly state four lines of argument, which I elaborate in more detail in the interpretative essay on the *Gorgias*.

First, then, the dialogue is named for the rhetorician Gorgias, even though he speaks a good deal less than, for instance, Callicles. Could this

---

30. Plato, *Republic* 1.327c.
31. Brian Vickers for example follows many others in saying that the "real subject" of the dialogue is "the rival claims of politics and philosophy to represent the good life" (*In Defence of Rhetoric*, p. 103).

not be because Gorgias is the most famous interlocutor? To be sure, but Plato does not always assign names in that manner: the dialogue on courage, for instance, is named the *Laches* not the *Nicias*. Furthermore, Gorgias's intervention is crucial for the dialogue's being carried through to a conclusion instead of breaking off unfinished. These facts suggest a close relation between the dialogue's theme and the rhetorician Gorgias.

Second, Socrates permits or rather compels the conversation to move from rhetoric to questions of justice and the best human life; yet on each occasion he makes the effort to bring it back to the subject of rhetoric—most notably, even in the closing myth about the soul's fate after death.

Third, near the beginning of the discussion (448d–e), Socrates distinguishes rhetoric from dialectic or conversation. He characterizes Polus's first speech about Gorgias's art as rhetorical, because it failed to say *what* the art is and instead said *what kind of* thing it is and praised it as if it had been attacked. Dialectic, we are left to presume, answers the question *what a thing is.* But when Socrates later overturns Polus's assertion that doing injustice without paying a just penalty is better than suffering injustice, the whole refutation turns on the premise granted by Polus (474c) that doing injustice is baser than suffering injustice; it rests, in other words, on an assertion of *what kind of* thing injustice is without making clear *what* it is. At this crucial point of the discussion, then, Socrates refutes rhetorically rather than investigates dialectically. May we not infer that Socrates is concerned with rhetoric to an exceptional degree in this dialogue?

Fourth, in his discussion with Callicles, Socrates is more openly self-conscious about persuasion, more explicitly concerned with his success or failure at persuading his interlocutor, than in any other dialogue, except perhaps the *Apology*. For instance, in driving Callicles from his position of immoderate hedonism (492d–499b), Socrates first evokes strange myths that confound life and death and compare the soul to a perforated jar. "Well, am I *persuading* you somewhat and do you change over to the position that the orderly are happier than the intemperate?" Socrates asks. When Callicles denies it, Socrates uses another likeness, of two sets of jars, and then again asks, "Do I somewhat *persuade* you . . . or do I not *persuade* you?" Next, Socrates tries to shame Callicles into abandoning his position by arguments about inflows and outpourings and the like. Callicles tells Socrates he should be ashamed of himself, Socrates returns the charge, but Callicles maintains his position. Socrates next tries an argument to show how our way of experiencing pain and pleasure differs from our experiencing of clearly good and bad things like health and sickness. Here Callicles becomes decidedly recalcitrant: he denies that he understands Socrates' "sophisms" and belittles

Socrates' kinds of questions and examples; he continues only in consequence of Gorgias's effective urging. When Socrates has completed *that* argument, he presents another, "for," he says, "I think it is not agreed on by you in this way." This other argument *does* finally lead Callicles to abandon immoderate hedonism, if with ill grace. The previous argument failed, it seems, because of its rather abstract, theoretical character. The last one works by linking the issue of the good and the pleasant to something that Callicles cares deeply about: the prudence and courage of the superior men.

What are we to make of these multiple attempts at persuasion? Socrates, it seems to me, experiments with, or demonstrates before Gorgias, various modes of persuasion. Socrates starts with what he does least well and ends with the dialectic that he is best at. Or one could say, he starts with the mode that could work best with large numbers of people and ends with what can work best with a given individual. For Gorgias, perhaps, the reverse order would hold: he could do best at elaborating the tales and images that Socrates presents flatly and ineffectively. Thus, I suggest, a possible division of persuasive labor between philosopher and rhetorician is provisionally sketched. Whatever merit that suggestion may have, the emphasis on persuasion and the concern with rhetoric clearly appear central to Socrates' proceedings.

When we turn to the *Phaedrus*, it is yet more problematic to determine the central theme. Indeed, the very being of the *Phaedrus* itself, as a written text, is perhaps the most striking irony in Plato's writings. We behold Socrates, who left behind no writing, denigrating the value of writing as such and arguing that a serious man can only regard his writings as playful side-occupations—and this we read written by Plato, in whom virtually every serious reader discerns a most careful and polished writer. We learn that a writing should have a unity like that of a living being, with all its parts suitably adapted to the whole; yet the unity of the *Phaedrus* is as hard to articulate as that of any dialogue in the whole Platonic corpus.

The central difficulty here, of course, is to understand just what kind of whole is constituted by the *Phaedrus*'s two main parts: speeches about love, and discussions of speech writing and rhetoric. Some ancient editor gave the *Phaedrus* the subtitle "On Love"; other ancient scholars, however, maintained that its chief subject was rhetoric. Hermias affirmed that it was "about the beautiful of all kinds."[32] A thoughtful and thorough recent book on the *Phaedrus* argues that the question of self-knowledge provides the

---

32. Hermias, cited in G. J. De Vries, *A Commentary on the "Phaedrus" of Plato* (Amsterdam: A. M. Hakkert, 1969), p. 22.

central and unifying theme.[33] In my own view, the recent commentator De Vries puts it about right. He asserts that rhetoric, or "the persuasive use of words," is the central theme, with beauty, knowledge, and love treated as topics intertwined with the inquiry into the foundations of persuasion.[34] In what follows, I try to lend further support to this position by showing how the *Phaedrus* and *Gorgias* complement each other so as to present Plato's full understanding of rhetoric.

THE TWOFOLD CHARACTER OF PLATO'S TREATMENT OF RHETORIC

I can state the gist of my view of the relation of Plato's two treatments of rhetoric in the form of a proportion: as the *Republic* is to the *Symposium*, so is the *Gorgias* to the *Phaedrus*; or equivalently, the *Gorgias* stands in relation to the *Republic* as the *Phaedrus* does to the *Symposium*. To restate this point in terms of central themes: the *Republic* deals with justice, the *Symposium* with *erōs* or love; the *Gorgias* treats rhetoric about justice, the *Phaedrus* rhetoric about love.

Before elaborating this point in regard to the different presentations of rhetoric in the *Gorgias* and *Phaedrus*, I need to sketch one general reflection on the character of each Platonic dialogue and on the relations between them, which I shall illustrate with a comment on the relation of the *Republic* to the *Symposium*. Each of Plato's many dialogues is decidedly one-sided or partial. It pursues a particular approach to an issue, or a limited aspect of an issue, or a special point of view on an issue; or it treats an issue with a view to meeting some particular human need in the circumstances; or in some other way it is particular, partial, limited in its scope. In consequence, if one is to understand Plato's thought fully, one needs to supplement what one sees in any single dialogue with what can be learned from other dialogues. Doubtless, complete understanding of Plato's thinking would require full knowledge of every dialogue and adequate reflection on their interrelations. Yet even if such knowledge is unavailable to us, one may nevertheless sensibly observe that in studying a given dialogue on one particular theme, one can often see some rather obvious reasons why another one or two or three dialogues are especially necessary to supplement the partiality of the given one.

---

33. Charles L. Griswold Jr., *Self-Knowledge in Plato's "Phaedrus"* (New Haven : Yale University Press, 1986.)
34. De Vries, *Commentary on the "Phaedrus,"* p. 23.

For example, in dealing with perfect justice and the best city, the *Republic* downplays, abstracts from, and rides roughshod over *erōs*.[35] In particular, the argument builds on an inadequately supported, at best provisional, assertion that spiritedness is superior to desire of all kinds, including erotic desire. Consequently, for understanding more fully this crucial dimension of the human soul, or of human nature, one is most emphatically directed toward the *Symposium* as the necessary supplement.

In spite of what I have just said, each dialogue by itself is a complete and complex whole; each dialogue's chief thrust and emphasis may be one-sided, but each does at least allude to what it mainly passes over or distorts. Thus even if we had no *Symposium* to read, we could (though with more difficulty and without the help of as full a treatment by Plato) at least discern from a careful reading of the *Republic* that the very *erōs* being by and large crushed for the sake of the perfect city does nonetheless have its higher aspects. Socrates does make clear, after all, that not only the tyrant but also the philosopher is defined by his *erōs*. He makes perfectly clear, too, that even the austere education of the guardians culminates in *erōs* of the beautiful.

With these general considerations in mind, let us consider how rhetoric is treated in the two dialogues. The *Gorgias,* within the context of its treatment of rhetoric, resembles the *Republic* in some crucial ways, most notably its downplaying of *erōs*. The *Gorgias* presents rhetoric as, almost by definition, addressed to many people in some kind of political gathering. Socrates contrasts rhetoric starkly with dialectic, the one-on-one conversational mode of proof that he practices. He emphatically states that he does not converse with the many. In fact, he presents himself overall as if quite ignorant of what rhetoric is and what it can do. For most of the discussion, Socrates pursues the inquiry in such a way as to narrow the subject matter with which rhetoric is concerned down to justice. He attacks existing rhetoric chiefly on the grounds of justice: rhetoric pursues pleasure through flattery rather than genuine good through justice. And he presents justice itself largely as the art of correct punishing by the constituted political/judicial authority, whereby the soul of the unjust man is cured of its illness. The principal cause of injustice comes to sight as immoderate, unchastened desires, so that the health of soul at which just punishment aims seems to be most clearly denominated as moderation or even austerity. The discussion emphasizes the harshness and the pain connected with just

35. Leo Strauss, *The City and Man* (Chicago: Rand McNally, 1964), p. 111.

punishment. The closing myth presents gods who judge and punish souls after death; in keeping with the earlier emphases, here too the vivid details chiefly involve painful punishments.

Although during much of the *Gorgias* Socrates attacks most rhetoric as flattery without genuine art, he nonetheless points toward the possibility of a true rhetoric, or a true political art, that would strive to make citizens more just and better. In criticizing actual statesmen like Pericles for lacking this art, Socrates uses the unstated premise that such an art would be all-powerful. But when he himself claims to be the only person who practices the true political art, Socrates admits that he has no political rhetorical effectiveness or political power in the usual sense, thus suggesting that this true political art is altogether without power. We are left to infer that a true rhetorical art devoted to promoting justice could have a measure of power lying somewhere between the extremes of all or nothing.

How sharply the *Phaedrus* contrasts with the *Gorgias*! At least as sharply, I venture to say, as the *Symposium* contrasts with the *Republic*. The dialogue takes place between two people outside the city walls, in contrast to the large gathering before whom Socrates converses with Gorgias and others. The *Phaedrus*'s discussion of rhetoric arises in connection with speeches about *erōs*; the substantive matters discussed are largely private, with only brief[36] references to anything political. Although of course never blaming moderation or sobriety, Socrates nonetheless presents a remarkable praise of *erōs* as a kind of divine madness. Socrates here is so far from rejecting long speeches, as he ostentatiously does in the *Gorgias*, that he describes himself as sick with desire for speeches and delivers one much longer than any in the *Gorgias*. Socrates shows himself to be very well informed about contemporary rhetoric. He criticizes that rhetoric not on the grounds of justice and politics, but for inadequately artful or scientific procedures. He does not explicitly discuss the question of rhetoric's power, but his own remarks on developing a proper art of rhetoric would seem to aim at, among other things, making it more reliably effective. When he develops his own notion of rhetoric, he does not limit it to political rhetoric, but suggests a universal art of *psychagōgia*, the leading of souls. The real art of rhetoric would not be something to be sharply contrasted with dialectic, but would

36. But not necessarily for that reason unimportant; the reference to lawgivers like Solon as writers, for instance, surely provides significant matter for reflection on what Socratic or Platonic rhetoric might aim at. Rhetoric combines with compulsory legislation in a noteworthy manner through the Athenian Stranger's proposal for persuasive preludes to laws (*Laws* 722d–724a).

need to be developed by a person skilled in dialectic, who made, concerning human souls and their actions and passions, all the synoptic definitions and the analytical divisions in accordance with the natural articulations of things necessary to develop a true rhetorical science. And certainly the philosopher would have a definite leg up on performing this work. The gods are no less present in the *Phaedrus* than in the *Gorgias*, indeed they are more so, but here they come to sight as objects of our *erōs* or rather as leaders of our endeavor to behold the truly beautiful.

How can two such disparate treatments be put together into a coherent whole that we may call Plato's understanding of rhetoric? Overall, the more closely one examines assertions made in each dialogue, with due regard to context and to various stated or implicit qualifications, the more one finds them to be not so much contradictory as complementary. To give one important example: rhetoric in the *Gorgias* comes to sight chiefly as political, which is taken to mean directed above all or even exclusively to the many. Because the most common source of political ills is immoderate desires, good rhetoric according to the *Gorgias* seeks above all to create order, geometrical proportion, harmony, and restraint in the souls of citizens; these traits are favored by the gods, who endorse human punitive justice and perfect it after death. The *Phaedrus*, on the other hand, deals chiefly with the few who especially give thought to speeches, among whom might be found those who could develop a true art of rhetoric. Like the *Gorgias*, the *Phaedrus* too favors order, harmony, and balance in the human soul; but it seeks to attain this goal chiefly through correctly directing the soul's erotic love (at best a type of divine madness) for the beautiful. People can acquire good order in their souls by being driven by fear, or drawn up by love; a philosophically developed rhetoric must understand and use both motive forces in their proper places. The philosophically minded person who might develop such rhetoric would be moved chiefly by love of the beautiful.

The Power of Rhetoric for Plato

The *Phaedrus* and the *Gorgias* complement each other in a most significant way in regard to the question of rhetoric's power. Let me begin to reflect on this question by asking: In what aspect of political activity would the philosopher have some advantage in practice? To put it most comprehensively, the philosopher's advantage must be that, unblinded by false opinions and spurious hopes, he can see most clearly and analyze most effectively any political situation.[37] However, political understanding of this kind does not yet amount to practical action. When it comes to such action, I suggest, the philosopher's chief advantage can be expected to lie in the area of rhetoric.[38] How great a political advantage, precisely, is that?

The Sophists, as characterized by Aristotle[39] and as exemplified in this respect for Plato by Gorgias, identify or nearly identify politics with rhetoric. As Leo Strauss puts it, "the Sophists believed or tended to believe in the omnipotence of speech." Xenophon, like Plato and Aristotle, rejected such a view of politics and rhetoric.

> Xenophon speaks of his friend Proxenos, who commanded a contingent in Cyrus's expedition against the king of Persia and who was a pupil of the most famous rhetorician, Gorgias. Xenophon says that Proxenos was an honest man and capable to command gentlemen but could not fill his soldiers with fear of him; he was unable to punish those who were not gentlemen or even to rebuke them. But Xenophon, who was a pupil of Socrates, proved to be a most successful commander precisely because he could manage both gentlemen and nongentlemen. Xenophon, the pupil of Socrates, was under no delusion about the sternness and harshness of politics, about that ingredient of politics which transcends speech.[40]

Can so intelligent a man as Gorgias, so aware of his own interests (and as we see in Plato's dialogue, so aware of dangers from cities hostile to his art of rhetoric), really have ignored this simple fact about the limits of speech's power in politics? In some sense, surely not. But perhaps the sophist—or as we might say, the intellectual—has two deep-seated tendencies: first, to overestimate the political advantage conferred by sharpness of mind; and, second, insufficiently to understand the necessary con-

---

37. Alexandre Kojève in "Tyranny and Wisdom" sketches three distinctive traits of the philosopher that constitute advantages over the "uninitiate": expertise in dialectic, discussion, argument; freedom from prejudices; and greater openness to reality and hence closer approach to the concrete (whereas others confine themselves more to abstractions, without "being aware of their abstract, even unreal character"); in Strauss, *On Tyranny*, p. 157.
38. Whether the philosopher chooses to put that advantage to use, and if so, how, are of course separate questions.
39. Aristotle, *Nicomachean Ethics* 10.1181a14–17.
40. Leo Strauss, "Machiavelli," in *Studies in Platonic Political Philosophy* (Chicago: University of Chicago Press, 1983), p. 228.

ditions for the pursuit of his own preferred activities. The former tendency was given a classic formulation by Hobbes, following Thucydides:

> Men that distrust their own subtilty, are in tumult, and sedition, better disposed for victory, than they that suppose themselves wise, or crafty. For these love to consult, the other (fearing to be circumvented,) to strike first. And in sedition, men being alwayes in the procincts of battell, to hold together, and use all advantages of force, is a better stratagem, than any that can proceed from subtilty of Wit.[41]

The latter tendency, likewise of central importance to Hobbes's thinking, was powerfully represented in Aristophanes' comic criticism of Socrates in the *Clouds*, where we see a Socrates whose all-absorbing interests in nature, in language, and in thought prevent his taking seriously the political and moral concerns of the community on whose continued stable and prosperous existence his own activity depended. Intellectuals today, I need hardly add, generally display no greater immunity to these two tendencies than they have in the past.

Plato, like Xenophon and Aristotle, is acutely aware of rhetoric's limited power in politics and reflects profoundly on the fact. But does he not agree with the sophistic rhetoricians at least so far as to recognize that artful persuasion can have great power? Are not the Sophists correct that, at least in normal circumstances, rhetoric plays a key role in gaining political office and in bringing about one result in a political deliberation (or in a judicial proceeding) rather than another? I believe that Plato would accept this assertion, but he would place greater emphasis than the Sophists do, in his understanding of politics, on what in any given situation limits the range within which rhetorical persuasiveness can have effect.

What the power of rhetoric can achieve at any specified time and place is limited in several ways. Most obviously, the dimension of force (and what may guide the use of force, such as passionate pursuit of one's self-interest) in politics limits what persuasion can accomplish: Polemarchus's suggestion that you cannot persuade those who will not listen remains forever relevant. No less important as limits are a society's existing authoritative opinions and prevailing beliefs. That dimension of political or social

---

41. Thomas Hobbes, *Leviathan*, ed. C. B. Macpherson (Harmondsworth: Penguin Books, 1968), p. 163; cf. Thucydides 3.83.3–4, which Hobbes paraphrases.

reality's limiting the power of rhetoric is what underlies Socrates' observation in the *Apology* that one way to persuade his audience would be easier than another (even though that other is true). The existing beliefs that are crucial in these respects involve people's ordering of the human goods (such as the relative worth of money, health, fame, virtue, knowledge), their views of what beings are higher than human beings and their affairs (the divine, god, or gods), and the relationships between these two sets of beliefs. In only one day, even the most skilled rhetor can hardly succeed in persuading people contrary to powerfully and deeply held beliefs.

But could not rhetoric have substantially greater power if persuasion is exerted over a much longer period of time? Could a long-term rhetorical effort over many generations bring about much greater effects through profoundly changing people's opinions and beliefs? The example of how later Greek thinkers understood Homer's influence illustrates the possibility of seriously entertaining such an enterprise. Socrates, for instance, speaks of "praisers of Homer who say that this poet educated Greece."[42] Plato, I suggest, intends just such an educational enterprise, under the direction, of course, of Socratic or Platonic philosophy.

The *Gorgias* makes clear the political and moral need for such a project of reforming prevailing beliefs and limns key features of the substance of preferable ones. The *Phaedrus* explores how to understand what can make rhetoric effective and hence how a philosophic art of rhetoric could be developed. The *Phaedrus* culminates in a discussion of writing because writing appears indispensable if an enterprise is to pursue a determined course over many generations. Thus Plato sketches the possibility of a prolonged rhetorical project conducted by philosophy for its own benefit as well as for that of political society. A philosophically inspired and directed rhetoric of this sort would be a political philosophy, which, for reasons that both the *Gorgias* and the *Phaedrus* help to clarify, may sometimes resemble mythology or theology. The thoughtful reader of the *Gorgias* will not likely be surprised to read in Plato's last and longest dialogue that the Athenian Stranger presents an extensive theology in the context of discussing penal legislation.[43]

42. Plato, *Republic* 10.606e.
43. Plato, *The Laws* 10.

Phaedrus

DRAMATIS PERSONAE: SOCRATES, PHAEDRUS

227a   SOCRATES: Phaedrus[1] my friend! Where to? And from where?

PHAEDRUS: From Lysias, Cephalus's son,[2] Socrates, and I am going for a walk around outside the wall; for I spent a long time there, sitting around since early morning. In obedience[3] to your comrade and mine, Acumenus,[4] I take walks along the roads; for he says they are

227b   more invigorating than those in colonnades.

SOC.: What he says, comrade, is fine. But then Lysias was in town, it would appear?

PHAE.: Yes, at Epicrates', in that house there, of Morychus's,[5] near the Olympian's temple.

---

1. Phaedrus appears in two other Platonic dialogues. He is the first speaker in the *Symposium*, and indeed, together with Eryximachus, the proximate cause of the whole evening's theme of speeches on erotic love. With Eryximachus and Andron son of Androtion (see *Gorgias* 487c), he appears among those listening to the Sophist Hippias in the *Protagoras*. Little else is known of the historical Phaedrus. The dramatic date of the *Symposium* is 416, of the *Protagoras* about 432. Lysias returned to Athens in 412–411 (at which time Isocrates would have been twenty-four years old); probably we should think of this dialogue as occurring about then.
2. The conversation presented in the *Republic* takes place at Cephalus's house in the Piraeus, the port belonging to Athens and connected to the central city by the long walls. His two sons were Polemarchus and Lysias, the famous Attic rhetor, some thirty of whose speeches have been preserved. Both are present in the *Republic*, but of the two, only Polemarchus speaks.
3. The passive participle of *peithein*, to persuade, conveys the idea "being persuaded by" or "obeying."
4. Acumenus, a doctor, is the father of Eryximachus, also a doctor.
5. Morychus was something of a byword in comedies (e.g., Aristophanes, *Acharnians* 887) for his luxurious living.

25

soc.: So what, then, was the pastime? Or is it clear that Lysias was feasting you with speeches?[6]

phae.: You will learn, if you have the leisure to listen as you walk on.

soc.: What then? Do you not suppose that I would deem it, with Pindar, a "more important affair than business"[7] to hear what your and Lysias's pastime was?

227c   phae.: Go ahead, then!

soc.: You may speak.

phae.: And indeed, Socrates, the hearing is befitting for you at least; for actually the speech that we were passing our time on was, in I know not what way, erotic.[8] For Lysias has written about an attempt being made on one of the beautiful ones;[9] but not by a lover—indeed this very thing is what he has put with subtle refinement. For he says that one must gratify the nonlover rather than the lover.

soc.: Nobly born man! Would that he had written that one must do it for the poor man rather than the rich, and for the older rather than

227d   the younger, and whatever other things pertain to me and to most of us! Then indeed the speeches would be urbane and beneficial to the people. As it is, I for one have conceived such a desire to hear, that if you proceeded to take your walk to Megara[10] and, following Herodicus,[11] you advanced to the wall and went back again, I would not get left behind you.

phae.: What are you saying, Socrates, you best of men? Do you sup-

6. Note the similar suggestion (that speeches are feasts) at the beginning of the *Gorgias*.

7. The quotation is from *Isthmian* 1. The poet declares his intention to interrupt his business of writing a poem in honor of the island of Delos, sacred to Apollo, in order to perform his patriotic duty of celebrating a local winner of the Isthmian Games. He begins: "My mother, Thebes of the golden shield, I shall make your affair more important even than business." The word translated "business" is *ascholia*, "lack of leisure" (used also in *Gorgias* 458c)

8. Socrates, though usually proclaiming his lack of knowledge, sometimes claims expertise regarding *erōs*, perhaps most notably at *Symposium* 177d–e. I have translated *erōs* and related words with "love" and related words; but "love" must also be used sometimes for words with the root *phil*-, like "love of wisdom" for *philosophia*. I have indicated such cases in the notes.

9. *Kalos* means "beautiful," "noble," "fine." I have used all three translations according to context. I have translated *gennaios* "nobly born" to preserve its etymological connection with birth, generation, descent.

10. Megara, adjacent to Attica and allied with Sparta, figured prominently in events leading to the outbreak of the Peloponnesian War.

11. Not Gorgias's brother, but according to Plato's Protagoras (*Protagoras* 316d–e) a contemporary Sophist from Megara who hid his wisdom under the guise of the art of gymnastic or physical training. In the *Republic* 406a–b he is blamed for too sophisticated a medicine combined with gymnastic that excessively prolongs life in sickness.

228a pose that what Lysias, the most terribly clever at writing of the men of today, has composed at leisure over much time, I, a mere layman,[12] shall recollect in a manner worthy of him? Far from it. And yet I should wish for this rather than that much gold should become mine.

soc. Phaedrus, if I fail to know my Phaedrus, I shall forget even myself. But neither of these is the case. Well do I know that, when that man heard Lysias's speech, he didn't hear it only once but often or-
228b dered him repeatedly to speak, and he obeyed eagerly. And even these things were not sufficient for him, but he ended up getting hold of the book[13] and looked over those things which he most desired; and sitting around doing this since early morning, he tired of it and went for a walk—knowing the speech by heart, as I think, by the dog,[14] unless it is quite long indeed. And he proceeded outside the wall so as to practice. Encountering the one who is sick[15] over hearing speeches, he saw—yes, he saw—and was pleased that he should
228c have the fellow Corybantic reveler,[16] and he ordered him to go ahead. And when the lover of speeches begged him to speak, he played hard to get as if not desiring to speak. But he was going to end up speaking—even by force, if someone would not willingly listen. So then, Phaedrus, beg him to do right now what he will do presently at all events.

PHAE.: Truly the strongest thing by far for me is to speak in whatever way I can, since you seem to me someone who will not at all let me go before I speak in some way or other.

soc.: Quite truly indeed do I seem so to you!
228d PHAE.: So that's what I'll do. For really, Socrates, it's above all that I have not thoroughly learned the words; but the thought of nearly all the respects in which he said that the things pertaining to the lover differ from those pertaining to the nonlover—I shall go through the chief points of each in succession, beginning with the first.

soc.: When you've first shown, friend,[17] what it is that you have in

---

12. *Idiotēs:* a private man, layman, amateur, as compared to a (public) expert or professional.

13. Or one could translate "scroll," which makes Socrates' remark at 228d more pointed.

14. At *Gorgias* 482b, Socrates indicates that this odd oath refers to an Egyptian god.

15. The metaphor of sickness for overpowering erotic desire is used often in what follows. So too at *Symposium* 207a–b, Diotima links being sick and being erotically disposed.

16. A Corybant is a dancer in an ecstatic mystery rite. Socrates makes a remarkable comparison of his own hearing of certain arguments to Corybantes' hearing of flutes, at *Crito* 54d.

17. More literally, "friendship." Socrates addresses Phaedrus here with the abstract noun.

your left hand under your cloak; for I am guessing that you have the
speech itself. And if this is so, think about me in this way: that while
228e   I love[18] you by all means, when Lysias too is present, it has not seemed
best[19] at all to provide myself for you to practice on. But come, show!

PHAE.: Stop! You have driven me away from the hope I had that I
should do my gymnastic exercise on you. But where do you wish us
to sit down and read?

229a   SOC.: Let us turn aside right there and go along the Ilissus, and then
we shall sit down in a quiet spot wherever it seems good.

PHAE.: Good timing, it seems, that I happened to be barefoot; you, of
course, always are. So it's very easy for us to go along the little brook,
getting our feet wet—and not unpleasant, especially at this season of
the year and hour of the day.

SOC.: Go ahead now, and at the same time look for where we shall sit
down.

PHAE.: Now, do you see that very tall plane tree?[20]

SOC.: Yes. Well?

229b   PHAE.: There is shade there, and a measured breeze, and grass to sit
on or, if we should wish, to lie down on.

SOC.: You may go ahead.

PHAE.: Tell me, Socrates, is it not from somewhere here along the Ilissus that Boreas is said to have snatched away Oreithyia?[21]

SOC.: He is said to have.

PHAE.: Well now, isn't it right here? Certainly the waters appear graceful, pure, and clear, and suitable for maidens to play beside them.

229c   SOC.: No; but some four or six hundred yards[22] farther down, where
we cross over toward the shrine in Agra. And a certain altar of Boreas
is there at that spot.

PHAE.: I've never quite noticed. But tell me, by Zeus, Socrates: are you
persuaded that this mythical speech is true?

---

18. Here Socrates uses the verb *philein*, related to *philos* (friend), not the verb *eran*. See first
note at 227c and *Gorgias* 513c and second note there.

19. This phrase is also used to speak of official decrees of the assembly. One could translate, "It has not at all been decreed." See *Gorgias* 466c and note there.

20. Given the Greek penchant for wordplay, it may be worth noting that "plane tree" translates *platanos*.

21. Boreas is the North Wind. Oreithyia was daughter to Erechtheus, a mythical king of
Athens.

22. Literally, two or three *stadia*. Agra is a *deme* or political subdivision of Attica. Herodotus
7.189 relates that the shrine to Boreas was built on the Ilissus after the North Wind destroyed the Persian fleet, in response to prayers by the Athenians to Boreas and Oreithyia.

soc.: Well if, like the wise, I distrusted it, I would not be out of place.[23] In that case, playing the sophist I would assert that Boreas's wind hurled her down from the nearby rocks where she was playing with Pharmaceia, and thus she ended up said to have been snatched
229d up by Boreas—or else from the Areopagus;[24] for this account in turn is also told, that she was snatched away from there, not from here. But I, Phaedrus, consider such things in other respects graceful, but belonging to a man who is too terribly clever, laborious, and not altogether fortunate, if only because it is necessary for him after this to straighten out the form of the Hippocentaurs, and next that of the Chimera; and then in will stream a mob of such Gorgons and Pega-
229e suses and multitudes of other inconceivable things and bizarre curiosities of certain natures of which marvels are told.[25] If someone, distrusting these, will make each thing approach near to what's likely, as if using a certain rude wisdom, he will stand in need of much leisure. But I do not at all have leisure for these things; and the cause of it, my friend, is this. I am not yet able, according to the Delphic inscription, to know myself;[26] it appears to me laughable indeed
230a for one who is still ignorant of this to examine alien things. Wherefore, bidding farewell[27] to these things and being persuaded by what is conventionally believed about them, as I was saying just now I examine not them but myself, whether I happen to be some wild animal more multiply twisted and filled with desire than Typhon,[28] or

23. *Atopos*, literally out of place or without a place; elsewhere I have sometimes translated it "strange" or "bizarre."

24. The Areopagus, or "hill of Ares (the god of war)," was a small hill on which sat the council and court of elders.

25. A Hippocentaur has the head, torso, and arms of a man joined to a horse's body. The Chimera combined the forms of lion, goat, and dragon. The Gorgons were three women with snakes in place of hair. Pegasus was a winged horse that sprang up either from the blood of Medusa (the most famous of the Gorgons) or from the stump of her neck after she was decapitated by Perseus. The hero Bellerophon rode on Pegasus in order to kill the Chimera.

26. This inscription (*gramma*) "Know thyself!" was, along with "Nothing too much," perhaps the best known at Delphi.

27. The Greek uses the verb *chairein*, connected to words translated "gratify" and "graceful" previously. See *Gorgias* 505d and 505c and notes there.

28. This giant, perhaps the most frightening monster found in Greek myths, had enormous strength and the head of a dragon and of one hundred snakes, all flashing fire; he was the last child of Earth, born after Zeus had overthrown the Titans and established his rule. Zeus had to defeat him and cast him underground to secure his own rule and the present order as we know it. (Hesiod, *Theogony* 820–85; Homer *Iliad* 2.782). The word *atuphos*, translated "without arrogance" at the end of the sentence, is cognate with the name for this giant. De Vries identifies this as "the first appearance of the etymological fancy which is rife in the *Phaedrus*."

a gentler and simpler animal, having by nature a share in a certain lot that is divine and without arrogance. But comrade, amidst the speeches—wasn't this the tree to which you were leading us?

230b PHAE.: Yes indeed, this is the one.

SOC.: By Hera,[29] the resting place is beautiful, to be sure! This plane tree is especially wide-spreading and tall, and the height and shade of the willow are altogether beautiful, and as its flowering is reaching its peak, it makes the place as sweet smelling as can be; and in addition the stream flows most gracefully under the plane tree with especially cool water, by the testimony of my foot. It seems likely, from the maidens and other statues, to be the shrine of certain nymphs

230c and of Achelous.[30] And further, if you wish, how lovely and particularly sweet is the fragrant good breeze of the place! It responds with a summery and clear echo to the chorus of cicadas. And the most subtle refinement of all is the grass, because it is naturally sufficient, on a gentle slope, for someone laying down his head to be in an altogether beautiful situation. So that your work of guiding strangers, Phaedrus my friend, has been the best.

PHAE.: But you, you amazing man, appear to be someone very much out of place! For as you say, you absolutely seem like some stranger

230d on a guided tour and not one of the country. To such an extent do you not go away from home, neither out of the town nor beyond the boundaries, and it seems to me you don't go outside the wall at all.

SOC.: Forgive me, best of men. For I am a lover of learning.[31] Now then, the country places and the trees are not willing to teach me anything, but the human beings in town are. But you in my opinion have found the drug for my trip out. For just as they lead hungry animals by holding out and shaking a young shoot or some fruit, so you,

230e stretching out in front of me speeches in books, will evidently lead me around all of Attica[32] and anywhere else you wish. So now then, having arrived right here at present, it seems good to me to lie down; and you, in whatever posture you consider easiest to read, assume it and read.

29. Hera, wife of Zeus, appears to be invoked in oaths most often by women.
30. Nymphs were various deities or spirits of streams, mountains, groves, and the like; Achelous was the oldest river god.
31. *Philomathēs*.
32. Attica is the territory of Greece consolidated under the political community of Athens.

PHAE.: Listen then!

You know about my affairs, and you have heard what, these things having come to be, I believe to be advantageous for us. And I deem
231a   it fitting to be spared the misfortune of not getting what I ask for on this account, that I do not happen to be in love with you.[33] For those people, when they have ceased from desire, repent the benefactions they have conferred; but for these there is no time in which it is to be expected that they should have second thoughts. For they confer benefactions in proportion to their own power, not from necessity but voluntarily, as they have best taken counsel regarding their own concerns. Furthermore, lovers examine both those of their affairs that have been badly managed on account of love and the benefactions they have conferred, and adding to the account the toils they have
231b   had, they consider they have long ago paid back to the beloveds the favor in its worth. But nonlovers cannot on this account allege as a pretext the neglect of their own concerns, nor calculate past toils, nor blame differences with relatives on this; so that, with such great evils stripped away, nothing remains but eagerly to do whatever they think will provide gratification when they have done it. Furthermore,
231c   if it is worthwhile to make much of lovers on this account, that they claim they are most friendly[34] to the ones they love and are ready, in their speeches and in their deeds, to incur the hatred of others in gratifying the beloveds, it is quite easy to know, if they speak the truth, that they will make more of those with whom they fall in love later than of these, and it is clear that, if it seems good to those, they will treat these badly. And further, how is it reasonable to give over an af-
231d   fair of this sort to someone having a misfortune such as this, which no one of experience would even attempt to turn aside? For even they themselves agree that they are sick rather than of sound mind,[35] and know that they are thinking badly but have not power to master themselves. So how, then, when they are thinking well again, could they consider those things to be in fine shape, concerning which they

33. More literally, "to be a lover of you."
34. Here "to be friendly" translates the verb *philein*, for which one might choose "to love"; but I am using this latter for *eran*.
35. The word *sophrōnein* has a broad range of meanings, from "think soundly" to "be of sound mind" or "be moderate." See *Gorgias* 489e and 507a and notes there.

take counsel when thus affected? In addition, if you should choose the best one from the lovers, your selection would be from few; but if you should choose the most suitable one for yourself from the others,

231e   the selection would be from many, so that there is much greater hope that one worthy of your friendship happens to be among the many.

But if you're afraid of the established law,[36] lest reproach befall you

232a   when human beings hear of it, it is likely that lovers, thinking they should be held worthy of emulation by others too, just as they are by themselves, would be excited to speak and in their love of honor[37] would display before all that they have not toiled in vain; but non-lovers, being masters of themselves,[38] choose what is best instead of reputation among human beings. Furthermore, many must of necessity hear of and see the lovers following after the beloveds and mak-

232b   ing this their business, so that whenever they behold them conversing with each other, they suppose them then to be associated in the desire that has come to pass or that is about to be; but they don't even try to attribute blame to nonlovers on account of the association, knowing that it's necessary to converse with someone either for friendship or for some other pleasure. In addition, if fear presents itself as you think how it's hard for friendship to endure and that when a disagreement

232c   has arisen in any other way the misfortune is common to both, but when you have given over what you make very much of, great harm befalls you—then you should in all probability fear the lovers more. For many are the things that pain them, and they believe that all things that happen tend to their own harm. Therefore they even prevent the beloveds' associations with others, fearing that some who have acquired property may surpass them in possessions, that others who have gained education may prove to be stronger in intelligence;

232d   and they guard against the power of each one of those who have acquired some other good thing. So when they have persuaded you to be hated by these, they set you down in a solitude bereft of friends; but if, looking out for your own, you have a better thought than they, you will come into a disagreement with them. Those, however, who

---

36. The word *nomos* means law; custom; established institution, practice, or opinion. See *Gorgias* 482e and note there. Here one should probably take it in the sense of unwritten law or custom.
37. *Philotimoumenous*: another "*phil*- word" whose translation includes "love."
38. More literally, "being stronger than themselves." See *Gorgias* 482b and 488d and notes there.

happened not to be lovers but achieved through virtue what they asked for, would not be jealous of those who associate with you but would hate those who do not want to, supposing that they are despised by those, but benefited by your associates. So that there is
232e much greater hope that friendship rather than enmity will come to pass for them from the affair.

In addition, many of the lovers desire the body before they come to know the character and gain experience of the other personal traits, so that it's unclear to them whether they will still wish to be friends then,
233a when they have ceased from desire. But as for the nonlovers, who were friends with each other even before they did these things, it is not likely that these things, through which they received benefit, should diminish friendship with them; but these things are left behind as reminders of those that are going to be. In addition, it is to be expected that you would become better by being persuaded by me rather than by a lover. For those people praise the sayings and the doings[39] even contrary to what's best, in some cases fearing lest they be hated, in
233b other cases because their own knowledge is worse on account of desire. For love displays effects of the following sort: when they are unfortunate, it makes them believe that things that cause no pain to others are grievously distressing; when they are fortunate, it compels even things not worthy of pleasure to meet with praise from them. So that it is much more fitting for the beloveds to pity than to emulate them. But if you are persuaded by me, first, in my association with you
233c I shall attend not to present pleasure, but also to the benefit that lies in store for the future; I'll not be worsted by love, but in mastery of myself; and I shall not on account of small things take upon myself strong enmity, but on account of great ones shall slowly feel slight anger, forgiving involuntary things while trying to turn aside voluntary ones: these are testimonies of a friendship that will exist for a long time. Now if this thought presents itself to you, that strong friendship cannot come into being unless someone happens to be in love, you must
233d ponder in your heart that we would not make much of sons, nor of fathers and mothers, nor would we have acquired trusty friends, who have become such not from desire of that sort but from other practices.

Furthermore, if one must most gratify those who are most in need,[40]

---

39. That is, of the beloved.
40. Or "who ask (for it) the most."

it would be fitting in other respects too to confer benefits not on the best but on those most lacking resources; for, released from the greatest evils, they will acknowledge the most gratitude to them. Yes in-

233e deed, and in private feasts it's worthwhile to invite not friends but beggars and those needing replenishment; for they will appreciate and follow after and come to one's doors, and will be most pleased and will acknowledge by no means the least gratitude and will pray for many good things for one. But perhaps it is fitting to gratify not those most acutely in need,[41] but those most capable of returning the

234a favor; and not only those who are in love,[42] but those worthy of the affair; and not those who will enjoy your youthful beauty, but such as will give a share in their good things to you as you become older; and not those who, having accomplished it, will take pride[43] in it before others, but such as, with a sense of shame, will keep silence before all; and not those who pay serious attention for a short time, but those who will be friends equally through the whole of life; and not those who, ceasing from desire, will seek a pretext for enmity, but those

234b who, when the bloom of youth is passed, will then display their own virtue. Remember, then, the things that have been said and ponder this in your heart, that the friends of lovers admonish them on the grounds that the practice is a bad one; but no one of their kin has ever yet blamed nonlovers on this account for deliberating badly concerning themselves.

Perhaps then you might ask me whether I am recommending that you gratify all the nonlovers. Now, I suppose that neither would the

234c lover bid you to have this intention toward all the lovers. For, neither for him who gets it would it be worthy of equal gratitude, nor for you who wish to escape the others' notice would it be possible in like manner. Indeed, no harm must come about from this, but benefit for both. Now then, I believe the things I've said are sufficient; but if you long for something that you consider to have been left out, ask!

How does the speech appear to you, Socrates? Hasn't it been stated extraordinarily[44]—both in other respects and especially in its diction?

41. Or "those who ask most vehemently."
42. J. Burnet, *Platonis Opera*, Oxford Classical Texts, vol. 2 (Oxford: Clarendon Press, 1901) accepts Ast's conjecture instead: "those who beg."
43. *Philotimeisthai:* see first note at 232a.
44. *Huperphuos:* it is worth noting the root *phu-* (growth, nature) in this word; one might capture that connection by translating "preternaturally."

234d soc.: Indeed, demonically, comrade, so that I'm struck senseless! And I suffered this on account of you, Phaedrus, as I looked off upon you, in that you seemed to me, in the midst of reading, to brighten[45] under the influence of the speech; for, supposing you more than me to understand about such things, I followed you, and following I joined in Dionysiac revelry[46] with you, divine head.[47]

PHAE.: Let it be. So this, then, is how it seems good to play around?

soc.: Why, do I seem to you to be playing around and not to have been serious?

234e PHAE.: No, no, Socrates. But by Zeus the god of Friendship, tell me truly: do you think any other of the Greeks could say different things, greater and more profuse than these, about the same affair?

soc.: What then? Must the speech be praised by me and you not only because each of the words are clear, compact, and precisely turned on the lathe, but also on the grounds that its maker has said the needful things? For if it must be, I must yield for your sake, since it surely es-

235a caped my notice, because of my nothingness; for I applied my mind to its rhetorical aspect alone, and I didn't think that even Lysias himself thought this to be sufficient. In fact, Phaedrus, unless you say otherwise, he seemed to me to have said the same things two or three times, as if not altogether well provided with resources to say many things about the same subject, or perhaps as if he had no concern for such a subject; and certainly he appeared to me to act like a youth, showing off his ability to say it very well in both ways, saying the same things first one way and then another.

235b PHAE.: What you say is nothing, Socrates. For this very thing is what the speech most of all has got. For of the things inherent in the affair that are worth stating, it has left out nothing. So that besides the things said by that man, no one could ever say other things more profuse and worth more.

soc.: On this I shall no longer be able to be persuaded by you. For ancient and wise men and women who have spoken and written about these things will refute me, if I yield to gratify you.

45. De Vries points out the play upon Phaedrus's name (*phaidros*, meaning bright, beaming, joyous).

46. A more general verb here echoes the more specific Corybantic revelry of 228b–c.

47. This phrase "divine (*theios*) head" should perhaps remind us of Achilles' addressing the ghost of Patroclus as "honored (*ētheïē*) head" at *Iliad* 23.94. When Socrates addresses Phaedrus "dear head" at 264a, he repeats, as De Vries notes, the Homeric phrase "Teucer, dear head" (*Iliad* 8.281), spoken by Agamemnon to Telamon's bastard son (and half brother of Ajax).

235c   PHAE.: Who are these people? And where have you heard things better than these?

SOC.: Well, I cannot say now, just like that; but it's clear that I have heard from some people, either from the beautiful Sappho, maybe, or the wise Anacreon,[48] or perhaps from some writers. Now, judging from what do I say this? With my breast somehow full, demonic one, I feel that I could say, besides these things, others that are not worse. Now then, I know well, being conscious of my own lack of learning, that I have thought of none of these things by myself. It remains then,

235d   I suppose, that I have been filled like a jar through hearing from alien sources somewhere. And again from dullness I have forgotten this very thing too: how and from whom I heard them.

PHAE.: Yes indeed, most nobly born man, what you have said is very fine. And I shall not bid you to tell me from whom and how you heard. But do this very thing you are saying: you have promised to say other better and no less profuse things than those in the book, abstaining from them; and to you I promise, just like the nine archons,

235e   to set up in Delphi a golden image of equal measure,[49] not of myself only but also of you.

SOC.: You are most dear[50] and truly golden, Phaedrus, if you suppose I am saying that Lysias has missed the mark in every way and that I can really say things different from all these. This, I think, not even the paltriest writer would suffer. For example, take what the speech was about: who, do you suppose, saying that one must gratify the

236a   nonlover rather than the lover, would pass over lauding the one's prudence and blaming the other's folly, these being necessary in any case, and then would have some different things to say? Rather, I suppose that such things must be allowed and pardoned the speaker. And of such things it is not the discovery but the arrangement that is to be praised; of things that are not necessary but are difficult to find, in addition to the arrangement, the discovery as well.

PHAE.: I concede what you're saying; for in my opinion you have spo-

---

48. Sappho, born on the island of Lesbos about 140 years before Socrates, wrote mostly lyric poetry, especially on topics relating to love. Anacreon, likewise a lyric poet, was born about forty years later than she.

49. The archons in Athens took an oath to set up a statue of gold if they transgressed the law. "Of equal measure" translates *isometrēton*, which probably means life-size, but could mean of equal weight.

50. The word is the superlative of *philos*, "friend, friendly" (active sense) or "dear, loved" (passive sense).

ken in a measured manner. So then I too will act in this way: I shall
236b grant you to set down the lover's being more sick than the nonlover,
and you, having said of the remaining matters other things more profuse and worth more than those, you shall be set up wrought with
the hammer at Delphi, next to the Cypselids' votive offering.[51]

soc.: Have you taken serious offense, Phaedrus, because in joshing
you I attacked your boyfriend, and do you really suppose that I shall
attempt to say something different and more multicolorful, to put beside that one's wisdom?

236c PHAE.: As to this, my friend, you've got into the same sort of wrestling
holds. Now more than anything you must speak in whatever way
you can; but beware that we're not forced to do the tiresome business
of the comedians, answering back to each other, and don't wish to
force me to say that well-known "If, Socrates, I fail to know my Socrates, I shall forget even myself," and "He desired to speak, but
played hard to get." But think it over that we shall not go away from
here until you speak the things you said you have in your breast. We
236d two are alone in solitude, I am stronger and younger, and from all
these things "understand what I say to you,"[52] and don't in any way
wish to speak in consequence of violence rather than willingly.

soc.: But, blessed Phaedrus, I shall be laughable, a layman speaking
offhand about the same things, compared with a good writer.[53]

PHAE.: Do you know how things stand? Stop playing coy[54] with me! For
I have something to say by which I'll more or less compel you to speak.

soc.: Then don't say it at all!

PHAE.: But yes! I am saying it right now, and my speech will be an
oath.[55] For I swear to you—by which one, then, by which of the
236e gods? Or do you wish by this plane tree here?—yea verily, if you do
not say the speech to me opposite this very tree, never again shall I
either display or report to you any other speech of anyone.

---

51. Knowledge of that offering is not available. B. Schweitzer's *Platon und die bildende Kunst der Griechen* (1953), cited by De Vries, suggests that a golden statue of Zeus stood nearby; Phaedrus thus escalates the prize from a statue of Socrates next to one of himself to a statue of Socrates next to Zeus.
52. The words are quoted from Pindar (frag. 94 Bowra, 105 Snell, 121 Turyn), quoted too at *Meno* 76d.
53. The word *poiētēs*, here rendered "writer," was translated more literally "maker" at 234e6; it can also mean "poet."
54. *Kallōpizō:* more literally, "beautify the face."
55. A reminiscence of Achilles' angry speech to Agamemnon in Homer's *Iliad* 1.239.

soc.: Oh my, foul wretch! How well you have found out the necessity for the man who is a lover of speeches[56] to do what you bid!

PHAE.: So then what's with your twisting and turning?

soc.: Nothing more, now that you have sworn these things. For how should I be able to abstain from such a banquet?

237a   PHAE.: Then speak!

soc.: Well, do you know how I'll do it?

PHAE.: In what respect?

soc.: I shall veil myself to speak, so that I may run through the speech as quickly as possible and may not be at a complete loss from a sense of shame as I look toward you.

PHAE.: Just speak, and in other respects do as you wish!

soc.: Come then, Muses, whether you are named clear-toned[57] on account of the form[58] of your song or you have this surname on account of the musical race of the Ligurians, "Take part with me" in the tale, which this best of men here forces me to speak, so that his comrade,

237b   who even earlier seemed to him to be wise, now will seem yet more so.

Once upon a time there was a very beautiful boy, or rather youth, who had a great many lovers. A certain one of them was wily and, while no less in love than anyone, had persuaded the boy that he did not love him. And then came a time when, in making his demand, he was persuading him of this very thing, that he ought to gratify the nonlover in preference to the lover, and he spoke as follows:

Concerning everything, my boy, there is one ruling principle[59] for

237c   those who are to deliberate finely. One must know that which the deliberation is about, or else one necessarily misses the mark altogether. But it escapes the notice of the many that they do not know the being of each thing. And so, on the grounds that they know, they do not work out an agreement in the beginning of the investigation, but by going on ahead they pay back what's likely—for they agree neither with themselves nor with each other. So let us, you and me,

---

56. *Philologos.*

57. Greek *ligeiai.*

58. *Eidos,* "form," and *idea,* which I simply transliterate "*idea,*" both arise from the root that denotes seeing. See *Gorgias* 454e and note there.

59. The word *archē,* here translated "ruling principle," can mean simply "beginning" and also "rule."

not suffer what we censure in others. But since the argument lies before you and me as to whether one should enter into friendship rather with lover or with nonlover, having by agreement set down a
237d definition concerning love, as to what kind of thing it is and what power it has, let us look off to and refer to this as we make our investigation into whether it provides benefit or harm. Now then, that love is a certain desire is clear to everyone; and further, that nonlovers too desire beautiful things, we know. By what, then, shall we separate the lover and the nonlover? We must further observe that in each of us there are some two ruling and leading *ideas,* which we follow wherever they lead: the desire of pleasures that is naturally planted in us, and another acquired opinion that aims at the best.
237e These two things in us sometimes are of one mind, but sometimes they engage in factious struggle; and at one time the one, at another time the other, wins mastery. Now then, when opinion leads with reason toward the best and wins mastery, the name of the mastery is
238a *moderation;* but when desire without reason drags us toward pleasures and rules in us, the name *wanton outrage*[60] is applied to the rule. Wanton outrage, now, has many names—for it has many limbs and many forms[61]—and whichever of these *ideas* happens to become conspicuous causes the one who has it to be named by its own name, some name neither beautiful nor very worthy to have acquired. For when desire concerning food wins mastery over the reasoned ac-
238b count of what's best and the other desires, it is called mad gluttony and causes him who has it to be called this same thing. And again, when desire concerning strong drink tyrannizes, leading him who has acquired it in this direction, it is clear what epithet he will meet with. And as for the other names that are brothers of these, and names of brother desires, each time one rules as potentate, it's clear in advance how it is fitting to be called. On what account all the foregoing things have been said is already nearly evident, but what is stated is altogether clearer than what is unstated.[62] So then, the desire without reason which masters the opinion striving toward
238c what's correct and is led toward the pleasure of beauty, and which,

60. The Greek *hubris* covers a wide range of meanings: arrogance, violence, outrage, wantonness, lust, insolence, lewdness.
61. Another manuscript reads "many parts" instead of "many forms."
62. Several manuscripts read *pan pōs* instead of *pantōs:* "every thing that is said is somehow clearer than what is not said" (perhaps a proverbial saying).

in turn mightily gaining strength from desires that are akin to itself toward the beauty of bodies, conquers in its leading, taking its name from this very might, is called *love*.[63]

But Phaedrus, my friend, do I seem to you, as to myself, to have suffered some divine experience?

PHAE.: Absolutely, Socrates; contrary to custom a certain good fluency has possessed you.

238d   SOC.: Hear me, then, in silence. For really the place is like to be divine; so that if as the speech proceeds I should perchance become possessed by nymphs, don't wonder. For the things I am now giving voice to are no longer far from dithyrambs.

PHAE.: What you're saying is very true.

SOC.: And really, you are the cause of these things. But hear the remaining things; and perhaps, then, what is coming upon me may be turned away. These things, then, will be a concern for god; as for us, we must go back in speech to the boy.

So be it, most brave one.[64] What it happens to be that we must deliberate about, has been stated and defined. Looking toward it, as re-
238e   gards what remains let us say what benefit or harm from lover and from nonlover will likely come to pass for him who gratifies. Now, one ruled by desire and a slave to pleasure must necessarily, I suppose, make preparations for the beloved to be as pleasant as possible for himself; and to the sick person everything that does not resist is
239a   pleasant, while what is stronger[65] or equal is hateful. The lover will not willingly bear with either a stronger or an equal boyfriend, but always works to make him weaker and more deficient. Now, unlearned is weaker than wise, cowardly than courageous, incapable of speaking than rhetorical, slow than of ready wit. When so many and still more evils, as far as intellectual capacity goes, come into being and by nature exist in the beloved, the lover must necessarily be pleased by the ones and prepare to bring about the others, or else be

63. This definition of love, *erōs*, includes much wordplay involving the sound *rho* in the words for strength, might, etc.

64. De Vries notes that this epic term, used also twice in tragedy, may well convey an element of parody.

65. *Kreittōn* and *hēttōn*, in this passage rendered "stronger" and "weaker," also have the more general sense of "better" and "worse" or "superior" and "inferior." See *Gorgias*, note at 482b.

deprived of what is immediately pleasant. And he must necessarily
239b be jealous, and by keeping him away from many associations, especially beneficial ones from which he might become a real man,[66] he
must necessarily be the cause of great harm—of the greatest harm by
keeping him from the association from which he might be most intelligent.[67] And this happens to be divine philosophy, which the lover
must keep his boyfriend far away from, since he's terribly afraid of
being despised; and he must devise the other things so that the
beloved will be ignorant of everything and in everything look toward
the lover, and as such the beloved would be most pleasant to him,
239c but most harmful to himself. So then, concerning what pertains to intellectual capacity, the man in love is in no way profitable as trustee
and partner.

After these things we must look at the body's condition and treatment: What sort is it, and how will he give treatment to the one he's
gained authority over—he who has been compelled to pursue pleasant instead of good? He'll be seen pursuing someone soft and not
solid, reared not in pure sunlight but under mixed shade, inexperi-
enced in manly toils and hard sweat but experienced in a delicate
239d and unmanly way of life, adorned with alien colors and ornaments
for want of his own, practicing all the other things that follow along
with these, which are clear and not worthwhile to proceed further
with, but it's enough that, having defined one chief point, we go on
to something else: A body such that, in war or in other times of need
that are great, enemies take confidence, and friends and indeed the
lovers themselves feel fear.

This matter we must now let go as clear and must then say what
239e comes next: What benefit or what harm for us, as regards possessions, will the intercourse and trusteeship of the lover provide? This
at least is quite evident to everyone (and most so to the lover): that
he would pray above all that the beloved be bereft of the most
friendly, best-disposed, and most divine possessions; for he would
accept the beloved's being deprived of father, mother, kin, and friends,
240a considering them hinderers and censors of the most pleasant intercourse with him. But now, if the beloved has an estate of gold or of

66. The Greek *anēr*, here translated "real man," (and at 239c1 simply as "man") designates
a male human being and often suggests excellence in distinctively male respects like
courage (*andreia*). The generic term for human being is *anthrōpos*.
67. *Phronimos* means intelligent, prudent, sensible, practically wise. See *Gorgias*, second
note at 489e.

some other property, he will consider him neither equally easy to catch nor, when caught, as easily manageable; wherefore there is every necessity that the lover must be jealous of the boyfriend's having acquired an estate, and rejoice when it's destroyed. And so, furthermore, the lover would pray that his boyfriend be unwed, childless, without a household, for as long a time as possible, desiring to reap what is sweet for himself for as long a time as possible.

Now, there are other evils too, but some demon mixed pleasure for 240b the immediate moment with most of them. For instance the flatterer, a terribly clever beast and a great harm—all the same nature mixed in a certain pleasure that is not unmusical. And someone might blame the courtesan as harmful, and many other creatures and practices with ways of that sort, which for the day can be very pleasant. But for the boyfriend, the lover tends to be harmful and is the most 240c unpleasant thing of all to pass the day with. For as the ancient saying goes, one of the same age delights another—for I suppose that equality of time leading them to equal pleasures through similarity provides friendship—but all the same, even the association of these has its satiety. And indeed what is compulsory in everything is said furthermore to be grievous for everyone; now, in addition to dissimilarity, this most of all characterizes the lover in relation to the boyfriend. For the older man associating with the younger is willing to be left 240d behind neither night nor day, but is driven by necessity and frenzy[68] that leads him by always giving him pleasures, as he sees, hears, touches, and senses the beloved with every sensation, so that it is with pleasure that he serves the beloved closely. But as for the beloved, by giving what exhortation or what pleasures can the frenzy cause him, associating with the lover for this same time, not to reach the utmost point of unpleasantness—as he sees an older face, and not in the bloom of youth, with the other things that follow along with this, 240e which are not very delightful even to hear in speech, not to mention the ever-pressing necessity to manage them in deed; as he is kept under guard with guards that spy out evil all the time and toward everyone; as he hears untimely and excessive praises, and in the same way reproaches that are not bearable when the lover is sober, but when he has got into strong drink, shameful in addition to unbearable, as he indulges in tiresome and barefaced frankness?

68. *Oistros* can mean gadfly, stinging, frenzy, mad passion.

And while harmful and unpleasant when in love, when he has desisted from love he is not to be trusted in the time afterward, the time for which he made many promises with many oaths and bonds, so 241a that he barely effectuated, through hope of good things, toleration at that time of the burdensome association. But now that he ought to pay off, having changed to another ruler in himself and another leader, intelligence and moderation instead of love and madness, he has become other, which has escaped the boyfriend's notice. And the latter demands of him favor in return for the things of that time, reminding him of things done and things said, as if he's conversing with the same person; but from a sense of shame that one neither dares to say 241b that he has become other nor can he uphold the oaths sworn and the promises made under the earlier mindless rule, now that he has got possession of intelligence and has become moderate, so that he won't, by doing the same things as the earlier man, again become like that one and the same. Indeed he becomes a runaway from these things, and the former lover, having defaulted by necessity, when the shell fell differently,[69] changes and hastens to flight. The other is forced to pursue, vexed and hurling imprecations, having wholly ignored from the beginning that one should never gratify the lover who is of 241c necessity mindless, but much rather the nonlover who has intelligence; if not, one must of necessity give oneself up to someone untrustworthy, disagreeable, jealous, unpleasant, and harmful as regards property, harmful as regards the body's condition, and by far the most harmful as regards the soul's education, than which in truth, for both human beings and gods, there neither is nor shall be anything more honored. These things, then, you must meditate on, my boy, and know that the friendship of a lover does not come into being 241d with goodwill, but in the manner of food, for the sake of repletion, as wolves cherish lambs, so do lovers love boys.[70]

This is it,[71] Phaedrus. You may no longer hear me say anything further, but let the speech have this end for you.

---

69. The image refers to a game in which one team would pursue and the other flee, according to whether a tossed shell fell dark or light side up.
70. This line has dactylic hexameter meter, used in epic poetry. Plato probably has some proverbial saying in mind, though reference to *Iliad* 22.263 is possible. "Love" here is *philein;* "cherish" is *agapan*.
71. Socrates refers back here to his earlier stated fear that he would break out into poetry.

PHAE.: But I supposed it was in the middle, and would say equal things about the nonlover, how one ought rather to gratify him, telling in turn what good things he has. But as it is, then, Socrates, why have you left off?

241e SOC.: Didn't you perceive, blessed one, that I am already giving voice to epic verses and no longer dithyrambs—and this while blaming? If I should begin to praise the other one, what do you think I shall do? Don't you know that I shall be manifestly possessed by the nymphs, before whom you have thrown me with forethought? So then in one phrase, I say that whatever things we reviled in the one, the good things opposite to these belong to the other. And what need for a long speech? For what has been said about both is sufficient. And so

242a in this way the tale will suffer what it is fitting for it to suffer; and I shall cross this river and depart before I'm forced by you to do something bigger.

PHAE.: Not yet, Socrates, at least not before the scorching heat passes. Or don't you see that it's just now midday—high noon, as it's called? Instead, when we've waited around and at the same time conversed about what has been said, we'll go presently, when it cools off.

SOC.: You're just divine about speeches, Phaedrus, and simply[72] amazing. For I suppose that, of the speeches that have come into being in

242b your lifetime, no one has caused more to come into being than you, whether by saying them yourself or by compelling others in some one way—I take Simmias the Theban[73] out of the account; you dominate the others by very much—and now once more you seem to me to have become the cause of a certain speech's being spoken.

PHAE.: You are not declaring war, at any rate. But how, then, and what speech is this?

SOC.: As I was going to cross the river, good man, the demonic thing and the sign that customarily arises for me arose—and on each occa-

242c sion it holds me back from what I am going to do—and I seemed at that very moment to hear a certain voice, which is not allowing me to go away before I have made expiation, on the grounds that I have committed some fault toward the divine. I really am, then, a prophet, though not a very serious one, but just like those who are poor at let-

---

72. *Atechnōs*, "simply" or "absolutely," has the root meaning "without art."
73. He is most familiar to us from his crucial role, especially at 85c–d, in Plato's *Phaedo*, Socrates' discussion of the soul's immortality on the last day of his life.

ters,[74] I am just sufficient for myself alone. And so now I clearly do understand the fault. Since indeed, comrade, the soul too is something prophetic; for something disturbed me even as I was just now speaking the speech, and I was somehow put out of countenance, according to Ibycus, lest by "doing something amiss with the gods, I

242d should take in exchange honor from human beings."[75] And now I have perceived the fault.

PHAE.: What, then, do you say it is?

SOC.: Terrible, Phaedrus, terrible is the speech that you yourself introduced and forced me to speak!

PHAE.: How so?

SOC.: Simpleminded and somewhat impious; what speech might be more terrible than this?

PHAE.: None, at least if what you say is true.

SOC.: What then? Don't you consider Love to be from Aphrodite and to be a god?

PHAE.: So it is said, at least.

SOC.: But not by Lysias's or by your speech, which was spoken by you

242e through my mouth, when it had been bewitched by drugs. But if Love is, as so he is, a god or something divine, he would be nothing bad; but these two speeches just now spoke of him as being such. In this way, then, they were at fault about Love; and still their simplemind-

243a edness was quite urbane, while saying nothing healthy or true, to put on a solemn air as though they were something, if perchance by deceiving some little human beings they will enjoy good reputation among them. So then for me, friend, it is necessary to purify myself. For those at fault concerning the telling of tales there is an antique purification, which Homer did not know about, but Stesichorus did.[76] For having been deprived of his eyes on account of his evil-speaking about Helen, he did not ignore the cause, as Homer did, but, since he was musical, he knew it, and straightaway he composed:

---

74. *Grammata* could also mean writings; see note on *gramma* at 229e.

75. Ibycus was a lyric poet of the sixth century B.C. The *OCD* (*Oxford Classical Dictionary*; Oxford: Clarendon Press, 1949) describes him thus: "He has a rich and brilliant style, a vivid imagination, a great capacity for describing the emotions, especially love, and a real love of nature."

76. Socrates seems here to refer to a tradition that Homer was blinded for his speaking ill of Helen. Stesichorus was a lyric poet of the sixth century B.C.; the quotation is frag. 32 Bergk.

This speech is not genuine:
She did not go on the well-benched ships,
243b Nor did she come to Pergamon of Troy.

And having composed the whole *Palinode*, as it is called, he regained his sight on the spot. So then I shall turn out to be wiser than they in this very respect, at any rate: before suffering anything on account of my evil-speaking about Love, I shall try to give him back the palinode, with bare head and not, as then, veiled because of a sense of shame.

PHAE.: None of the things you've said to me, Socrates, are more pleasant than these.

243c SOC.: Indeed so, good Phaedrus, for you are reflecting on how shamelessly the two speeches were said, this one and the one pronounced from the book. For if someone of noble breeding[77] and gentle in character, who loved another such person or else had loved at some earlier time, happened to hear us saying how lovers take up great enmities on account of small matters and behave jealously and harmfully toward their boyfriends—how could you not suppose that he would consider he was hearing people who had been raised mostly among sailors and had seen no love worthy of free men,[78] and that he

243d would be far from agreeing with us on the things for which we blamed Love?

PHAE.: Perhaps so, by Zeus, Socrates.

SOC.: Accordingly I for one feel shame before this man and fear before Love himself, and so I desire to wash away with fresh speech the briny bitterness, as it were, of what we heard. And I counsel Lysias too to write as quickly as possible that in like ways[79] one must gratify the lover rather than the nonlover.

PHAE.: Know well, then, that so it will be. For when you have spoken the lover's praise, there is every necessity that Lysias will be com-

243e pelled by me to write in turn a speech about the same thing.

---

77. *Gennadas* used here is a Doric equivalent to *gennaios* (which I've translated "nobly born"; see *Gorgias*, note at 485d). The effect of this term may be subtly comic.

78. Literally translated: "free love."

79. Some translators, including R. Hackforth (Plato's "*Phaedrus*," [Translated with Introduction and Commentary] [Cambridge: Cambridge University Press, 1952]) and LSJ (*A Greek-English Lexicon*, by H. G. Liddell and R. S. Scott, new edition revised and augmented by H. S. Jones [Oxford: Clarendon Press, 1940; reprinted 1961]), take this phrase to mean "all things being equal."

soc.: In this I really put my trust, so long as you are who you are.

PHAE.: So then speak with confidence.

soc.: Where then is that boy of mine, to whom I was speaking?—so that he may hear this too, and not, unhearing, gratify the nonlover beforehand.

PHAE.: He is beside you, very near, always present, whenever you wish.

soc.: So then, beautiful boy, reflect in this way that the former speech
244a was that of Phaedrus, son of Pythocles, a Myrrhinousian man;[80] the one I am going to speak is of Stesichorus son of Euphemus, a Himeraian.[81] And it must be spoken as follows: The speech is not genuine which asserts that, when the lover is around, one must rather gratify the nonlover, on the grounds that the one is mad, the other of sound mind.[82] For if it were simply the case that madness is something bad, it would be beautifully said; but as things are, the greatest of good things come into being for us through madness, when, that is, it is given with a divine giving. For the prophetess in Delphi and
244b the priestesses in Dodona when mad have accomplished many beautiful things for Greece both in private and in public, but little, or rather nothing, when of sound mind. And if we should then speak of the Sibyl and others, who used divinely inspired prophesy to foretell in the future many things to many people and guide them aright, we would draw it out at length, saying things that are clear to everyone. The following is worth calling to witness: that those of the ancients who set down names also considered madness neither something
244c shameful nor a reproach; for they would not have woven this very name into the most beautiful art, by which the future is discerned, and called it "the manic art." But they set down its name with this belief, that it is beautiful when it comes into being by a divine allotment; but people today, with inexperience in beautiful things, throw on a *t* and call it "the mantic art."[83] And then too they gave the name

80. "Myrrhinousian" refers to Phaedrus's deme (a political subdivision of Athens; see *Gorgias* 495d); the formal mode of address creates, or perhaps satirizes, a solemn tone here.

81. The etymological elements of "Euphemus" make one think of "speaking well," the opposite of "blasphemy." "Himeraian" makes one think of the noun *himeros*, meaning longing, desire, love.

82. The same word, *sōphrōn*, has been translated "moderate" in other contexts. See *Gorgias* 489e and 507a (and notes there).

83. "The manic art" or art of madness translates *manikē*; "the mantic art" renders *mantikē*, elsewhere translated "art of prophesy" or divination.

"art of understanding-thought-information" [*oionoïstikē*] to the seeking of the future by people in their minds, who do it through birds and the other signs, seeing that from rational thinking they provide, through human understanding [*oiēsis*], thought [*nous*] and informa-
244d   tion [*historia*],[84] which the young today call "the art of bird augury" [*oiōnistikē*], making it more solemn with the long *ō*; so then, by as much as the art of prophecy is more perfect and more honored than the art of bird augury—the name more than the other name and the deed more than the other deed—by so much do the ancients testify that madness coming into being from god is more beautiful than soundness of mind from among human beings. And truly madness,
244e   springing up in and prophesying to those for whom it had to, found deliverance from the greatest sicknesses and toils, which were in certain families somehow from ancient guilts, by taking refuge in prayers to the gods and rituals, from which, happening upon purifications and rites, it put him who partakes of it out of danger for the present and the time thereafter, having found release from present
245a   evils for him who was correctly mad and possessed. And third, possession and madness from the Muses, seizing a tender and untrodden soul, arousing it and exciting it to a Bacchic frenzy toward both odes and other poetry,[85] adorns ten thousand works of the ancients and so educates posterity; but he who comes to poetic doors without the Muses' madness, persuaded that he will then be an adequate poet from art, himself fails of his purpose, and the poetry by the man of sound mind is obliterated by that of the madmen.

245b   So many, and still more, are the beautiful deeds of madness arising from gods that I can tell you. So let us then not fear this very thing, at any rate, and do not let some speech disturb and frighten us, saying that one must choose as friend, rather than him who has been moved, the man of sound mind; but let the latter carry off the prizes of victory only when he has shown, in the presence of the former, that love is not sent to the lover and the beloved from gods for their benefit. Now we in turn must demonstrate the opposite, that such mad-
245c   ness is given from gods for the greatest good fortune; and the demonstration will be untrustworthy for the terribly clever, but trustworthy

---

84. This kind of far-fetched etymology is found most abundantly in Plato's *Cratylus*. See the similar treatment of *erōs* at 238c.

85. *Poiēsis*, here translated "poetry," could well be translated "composition" and has also the more general meaning of "making."

for the wise. One must first, therefore, grasp in thought the truth about the nature of the soul, both divine and human, by seeing its experiences and deeds. The beginning of the demonstration is the following.

All soul[86] is deathless. For that which is always moving is deathless; and that which moves something else and is moved by something else, since it has a stopping of motion, has a stopping of life. Only that which moves itself, then, since it does not abandon itself, never ceases from moving, but this is also the source and beginning

245d of motion for whatever other things are moved. A beginning has no coming into being. For every thing that comes into being must of necessity come into being from a beginning, but the latter must not come from anything, for if the beginning came into being from something, it would no longer be a beginning.[87] And since it has no coming into being, it itself must of necessity be also incorruptible. For with the beginning destroyed, it will never come into being from something nor will anything else come into being from it, if indeed all things must come into being from a beginning. Thus, then, that very thing that moves itself is the beginning of motion. And this is not able either to be destroyed or to come into being, or else all the

245e heavens and all coming into being would collapse and stand still,[88] and would never again have the capacity to become moved. Now, since that which is moved by itself has been revealed as deathless, one will feel no sense of shame in saying that this very thing is the essence[89] and rational account of the soul. All body, indeed, to which being moved comes from outside is soulless; but all body to which being moved comes from within to itself from itself is ensouled, seeing that this is the nature of soul. If this is indeed the case, that that which

246a itself moves itself is nothing other than soul, soul would of necessity have no coming into being and be deathless.

So then, concerning its immortality, that's sufficient; but concern-

---

86. Taking *pasa* collectively; taking it distributively, "every soul. . . ."

87. This last clause translates Buttman's emendation, accepted by Burnet. De Vries prefers Hermann's construction of the leading manuscript reading, which would yield "it [viz., everything that comes into being] would not come into being as from a beginning [viz., beginning qua *the* first principle]."

88. "All the heavens" (or the whole heaven) here means something like the whole universe. Another reading, accepted by Burnet, would render: "the whole heaven and the whole earth would collapse into one and stand still."

89. *Ousia*, elsewhere translated "substance" or "being."

ing its *idea*, one must speak in the following manner. What sort of thing it is, is altogether in every way a matter for a divine and long narration,[90] but what it is like, for a human and lesser one; let us then speak in this manner. It is like some naturally conjoined[91] power of a winged team and a charioteer. Of the gods, then, the horses and charioteers are all good themselves and of good ancestry,[92] but as regards

246b   the others, there has been a mixture. And of us, first, the ruler holds the reins of the pair; and then of his horses, one is noble and good and of such ancestry, the other is of opposite ancestry and opposite; hard indeed and troublesome, of necessity, is the charioteering that concerns us. One must try to say how a living being[93] got called both mortal and deathless. All soul takes care of every soulless thing, and traverses all the heavens, at various times coming into being in vari-

246c   ous forms. And so when it is perfect and winged,[94] it travels on high and governs the whole cosmos,[95] but when it has lost its wings, it is borne on until it lays hold of something solid, and having settled down there and taken on an earthy body, which itself seems to move itself through the soul's power, the whole thing together, soul and body stuck fast, is called *living being* and has the surname *mortal*. What's called *deathless*, by contrast, is not from one rational account that's been figured out; but we fashion god, without either having

246d   seen or adequately perceived him in thought, as a certain deathless living being, which has a soul and has a body, with these naturally grown together for all time. But let these things be and be said in the way that is dear to the god; let us now grasp the cause of the wings'[96] being thrown off, through which they fall off the soul. And it is something of this sort.

90. Compare the "longer and further road" not taken, also about the soul, in *Republic* 435d. Consider too how importantly the capacity to use images or likenesses figures in this dialogue's later analysis of rhetoric.
91. Or more literally, "grown-together." Another manuscript reading would yield a different beginning of this sentence: "Let it be like a naturally conjoined. . . ."
92. More literally, "good and from good ones." This aristocratic formula (see "better and of better ancestry" at *Gorgias* 512d) is oddly thought-provoking as applied to gods.
93. *Zōon* is also the normal word for "animal."
94. Or one might translate, "full fledged." This and several other words with the root *pter* may involve the idea either of "wing" or of "feather." Thus just subsequent, "lost its wings" could be "lost its feathers," "molted." Wordplay on *ptero-* and *erōs* becomes explicit at 252b.
95. A possible alternate meaning would be "resides throughout the whole cosmos," that is, not fixed in one determinate location.
96. Or "feathers."

The wing's power naturally tends to lead what is weighty up, raising it on high to where the race of the gods dwells; and of the things
pertaining to the body, it most of all has in some way a common share
246e of the divine—and the divine is beautiful, wise, good, and everything of that sort. By these, then, is the soul's plumage most of all fos-
tered and increased; but by the ugly, bad, and the other opposites it
wastes away and is destroyed. The great leader in the heavens, Zeus,
driving a winged chariot, proceeds first, ordering and taking care of
all things; and an army of gods and demons follows him, ordered
247a into eleven parts. For Hestia alone remains in the gods' home.[97] Of
the other gods who have been ranged in the number of the twelve,
the rulers lead in the rank in which each has been ranged. So then,
many and blessed are the sights and pathways within the heavens,
along which the race of happy gods passes to and fro, each one of
them doing his own thing; and he who on each occasion is willing
and able, follows: for envy stands outside the divine chorus. And
247b then, when they go toward the feast and to the banquet, they proceed
uphill now to the summit of the arch under the heavens. The gods'
vehicles, in equal balance, being obedient to the reins, proceed easily;
but the others with difficulty: for the horse that has a share of badness is heavy, sinking toward the earth and weighing down the charioteer by whom he has been not beautifully reared. There indeed toil
and the ultimate contest lie before the soul. Now the souls that are
called deathless, when they have come toward the summit, proceed
247c outside and stand on the ridge of the heavens; and as they stand fast,
the rotation leads them around, and they see the things outside the
heavens.

As for the place above the heavens, no poet from among those here
has yet sung or ever will sing of it as it deserves. This is how it is—
for one must indeed dare to say what is true, especially when one is
talking about the truth—to wit, really existing being, colorless and
shapeless and impalpable, visible to the mind alone, the soul's helms-
man, with which the class[98] of true knowledge is concerned, occupies
247d this place. So then the thought of god, nourished with mind and un-
defiled knowledge, and the thought of every soul that is destined to
receive what is fitting, in time sees what is and greets it with affec-

97. Hestia, the goddess of the hearth, is often identified with the earth (De Vries cites in
particular Euripides frag. 944 Nauck).
98. *Genos*, translated previously as "race," e.g., of the happy gods.

tion, and looking at true things is nourished and feels good, until the rotation carries it around in a circle to the same place. And on the way round it beholds justice itself; it beholds moderation; it beholds knowledge, not that to which coming into being is linked, nor which is in some manner different when it is in respect of different things

247e   that we now call beings, but the knowledge that is in respect of what really is being. And in the same way having seen and feasted upon the other beings that really are, it sinks back into the place within the heavens and goes home. And when it has gone, the charioteer, stationing the horses before the manger, throws out ambrosia and gives in addition nectar to drink.[99]

248a   And this is the gods' life. Now, as for the other souls—the one that best follows and likens itself to god lifts the charioteer's head up into the place outside, and it is carried around with the rotation, thrown into confusion by the horses and with difficulty beholding the beings. Another soul at one time raises up, at another sinks down, and with the horses acting violently, it sees some things, but others not. And the other souls now, all eagerly longing for what is above, follow, but lack the power and are carried around together below the surface,

248b   treading on each other and jostling, one trying to get in front of another. So then confusion and conflict and the utmost sweat arise, where through the charioteers' badness many are maimed, and many have many wings broken. And despite their having much toil, all go away unfulfilled in respect to the sight of being, and having gone away, they make use of opinion for nourishment. For the sake of what, then, is it a matter of much seriousness to see there where the plain of truth is? It's both that the pasturage befitting what is best in the

248c   soul happens to be from the meadow there, and that the nature of the wing, by which the soul is lightened, is nourished on this. Now the following is Adrasteia's[100] ordinance. Whatever soul, having become a follower along with god, beholds something of the true things, shall be free of misery until the next[101] going around; and if it can always do this, it shall be always free of harm. But when, lacking the power to follow, it does not see and, having experienced some mischance, filled with forgetfulness and badness, it is weighed down, and hav-

99. This passage evokes Homer, *Iliad* 5.368f.
100. Another name (with the connotation "inescapable") for Nemesis, who punishes deeds of *hubris* (see 238a and note there), or for Necessity.
101. Or "second"; more literally, "other;" cf. the "third" at 249a.

ing been weighed down it loses its wings and falls toward the earth,
248d then the law is that this soul shall not on its first coming into being
implant in any bestial nature, but the one that has seen the most
things shall implant in that which will engender a man who will become a philosopher or lover of the beautiful or someone musical[102]
and erotic; the second in that of a lawful king or a warlike and com-
manding one; the third in that of a statesman[103] or some household
manager or businessman; the fourth in that of a lover of gymnastic
toil or someone who will be concerned with healing the body; the
248e fifth will have a prophetic life or a life occupied with mystic rites; to
the sixth, a poetic life or some other one of those concerned with imitation will be fitted; to the seventh, a craftsmanlike or farming; to the
eighth, a sophistic or demagogic; for the ninth, a tyrannical. Now in
all these, whoever passes his life justly receives a better allotment af-
terwards, and whoever unjustly, a worse. For each soul does not ar-
rive at the same place from which it has come for ten thousand
249a years—for it is not furnished with wings before so much time—
except for the soul of one who has philosophized without fraud[104] or
loved boys with philosophy; these souls, on the third thousand-year
way round, when they have chosen this life three times in a row, having thus been furnished with wings, go away on the three thousandth year. The other souls, when they have brought the first life to
an end, meet with judgment, and having been judged, some go to the
places of just punishment under the earth and pay off the just penalty;
the others go to a certain place of the heavens, having been lightened
by Dike,[105] and pass their time in a manner worthy of the life that
249b they lived in human form. In the thousandth year, both sets of souls,
arriving at the lottery and choice of the second life, choose the one
that each wishes. There it happens both that a human soul goes into
a beast's life and that one who was once a human being goes out of
a beast back into a human being. For at any rate the soul that has
never seen the truth will not come into this shape. For a human being must understand that which is said in reference to form, that

---

102. In the *Phaedo* (at 61a) Socrates reports his belief that philosophy is the greatest music.
103. *Politikos:* political man, politician, statesman; someone possessing competence in matters political.
104. Cf. *Gorgias* 451e and note there.
105. *Dikē*, the goddess Justice or Judgment, is the same word translated just previously as
"just penalty."

249c   which, going from many perceptions, is gathered together into one
by reasoning. And this is the recollection of those things that our soul
saw once upon a time, when it proceeded along with god and looked
down upon the things that we now assert to be, and lifted up its head
into the being that really is. And therefore, justly indeed, only the
philosopher's thought is furnished with wings; for through memory
he is always to the best of his power near those things, through being
near which god is divine. And the man who correctly uses such reminders, always fulfilling perfect rites—only he becomes really per-

249d   fected.[106] Standing back from matters of human seriousness and coming to be near the divine, he is rebuked by the many as moved out of
his senses, but that he is inspired by god[107] escaped the notice of the
many.

So then, here indeed comes to the fore the whole argument about
the fourth madness—madness, whenever someone, seeing beauty
here below and recollecting true beauty, is furnished with wings,
and, raising his new wings with eager striving to fly up, but lacking
the power, looking up after the manner of a bird but having no care

249e   for the things below, he takes the blame for being in a manic condition—that this, therefore, proves to be of all inspirations the best and
of the best ancestry, both for him who has it and for him who com-
municates a share of it, and that he who participates in this madness,
as one who loves the beautiful ones,[108] is called *lover.* For in accordance with what has been said, every soul of a human being by na-

250a   ture has beheld the beings, or it would not have gone into this living
being; but it is not easy for every soul to recollect those things from
the ones here—neither the souls that then saw the things there
briefly, nor those that fell hither and met with misfortune, so that under the influence of certain associations, turning toward what is unjust, they forget the holy things they saw at that time. Few, then, are
the souls that remain for which adequate memory is at hand. And
these souls, when they see some likeness of the things there, are astounded and no longer in possession of themselves, and they do not

106. "Perfected" or "fulfilled," or "initiated." The words translated "fulfilling," "perfect,"
"rites," and "perfected," all building on the root *tele-*, provide a notable play on words.
107. *Enthousiazōn:* a related noun is translated "inspiration" in the next sentence, 249e. At
241e Socrates' use of the same verb was translated more strongly as "possessed."
108. Or "beautiful things" (the gender could be masculine or neuter). "Lover," *erastēs,* is
perhaps suggested to have come from "loving" (*erōn*) and "best" (*aristēs,* applied to this
fourth madness).

250b   recognize what the experience is, on account of not perceiving with sufficient clarity. Now then, in the likenesses here of justice and of moderation and of the other things held in honor by souls, there is no splendor; but through dim organs, only a few people, with difficulty, going to the things' images, behold the kind of what is imaged. But at that time beauty was bright to see, when with a happy chorus they saw the blessed sight and vision—we following with Zeus, others with another of the gods—and accomplished that one of the rites that

250c   it is right to say is most blessed; a rite that we celebrated being ourselves whole and without experience of the evils which awaited us in later time, initiated into and as full initiates gazing in pure bright light upon whole, simple, calm, and happy appearances, we being pure and unmarked[109] with this thing we now, fettered in the manner of an oyster, carry around and name *body*.

So then let these things be a gracious tribute to memory, through which they have now been stated at rather great length, in yearning for the things of that time. As regards beauty, as we said, when it was

250d   with those things it shone forth, and we coming hither have seized hold of it as the most brightly glistening thing through the brightest of our senses. For sight comes to us as the sharpest of the senses that work through the body; but by it prudence is not seen—for it would produce terrible loves, if it presented some such bright image of itself to come to sight, and so would the other beloved things. But as it is, only beauty has this allotment, so as to be most manifest and loveli-

250e   est. Now then, he who is not newly initiated or has been corrupted is not quickly carried from here to that place toward beauty itself, when he has beheld its namesake here, and in consequence he does not feel awe as he gazes at it; but giving way to pleasure after the custom of four-footed beasts, he endeavors to mount and to sow children, and

251a   mingling with wantonness he feels neither fear nor shame at hunting pleasure contrary to nature. But the recent initiate, one of those who saw much at that time, whenever he sees a godlike face, or perhaps the *idea* of a body, that imitates beauty well, first he shivers[110] and something of the dreadful things of that time comes upon him; next, gazing at him he feels awe as before a god, and if he did not fear the reputation of excessive madness, he would sacrifice to the boyfriend

109. A mark, *sēma*, can also refer to a burial marker or tomb; hence the phrase may allude to the conception of the body as the soul's tomb (cf. *Gorgias* 493a).
110. De Vries notes that this wording may remind one of Sappho's famous poem; see 235c.

251b as to a statue and a god. And while he looks, a change, with sweat-
ing and unaccustomed heat, such as arises out of shivering, takes
hold of him. Receiving through the eyes the efflux of beauty, by which
the wing's nature is watered, he is heated; as he is heated, the parts
around where it would grow out, which, shut up with stiffness, formerly barred it from budding, melt; and as the nourishment flows in,
the wing's shaft swells and starts to grow from the root, under the
251c soul's whole form—for the whole soul was formerly winged. Hence
the whole soul boils in him and seethes. And the soul of him who is
beginning to grow wings experiences the same experience that happens around the teeth to those cutting teeth, when they are just growing them—itching and irritation around the gums: it boils and is irri-
tated and tickles around the growing wings. Now then, whenever
the soul, looking upon the boy's beauty and receiving particles that
come upon it and flow from there (indeed, on account of these things,
it is called "longing"),[111] is watered and heated, it abates from its dis-
251d tress and rejoices. But whenever it is apart and parched, the orifices
of the passageways where the wing starts, also dried up and closed,
shut off the wing's budding; each budding, shut off inside with longing and throbbing like pulsating arteries, pricks the passageway that
belongs to each, so that the whole soul, goaded all round, is stung
and distressed—but having memory afresh of the beautiful one, it rejoices. From both things being mixed together, it is sorely troubled by
the strangeness of the experience and, at a loss, is in a frenzy; and, be-
251e ing madly frantic, it can neither sleep at night nor remain wherever
it is by day, but it runs yearning wherever it thinks it will see the one
who possesses beauty. And seeing and letting the water of longing
pour in, it dissolves the things that had then been clogged up, and
catching its breath, is released from goads and pangs[112] and in turn
252a harvests in the present this sweetest pleasure. From this, to be sure,
it is not willing to be separated; nor does it make more of anyone
than of the beautiful one, but forgets mothers and brothers and all
comrades; and when its property is destroyed through neglect, it sets

111. "Longing," *himeros* (see second note at 244a) is fancifully derived here from *ienai* (to
go), *merē* (parts, here translated "particles"), and *rhoē* (flux). The terms used are characteristic of much pre-Socratic philosophy of nature or *phusiologia*, most notably Empedocles'
theory of light and vision.
112. This term is used most commonly of the pangs of childbirth; it is also applied, as here,
to love.

that down as next to nothing; despising all the conventional customs and graceful refinements, on which hitherto it prided itself,[113] it is ready to serve as a slave and to sleep wherever one allows, nearest its

252b yearning. For in addition to feeling awe at the one who possesses beauty, it has found him to be the only doctor for the greatest painful toils. This is the experience, beautiful boy to whom my speech is indeed directed, that human beings name *love*; but when you hear what the gods call it, you'll likely laugh on account of your youth. Some of the Homeridae,[114] I think, from the secret verses recite two verses about Love [*Erōs*], of which the second is quite outrageous and not very metrical. They sing thus:

Mortals call him flying Love [*Erōs*],
The immortals call him Winged [*Pterōs*], on account of wing-growing necessity.[115]

252c It is possible to believe these verses, and it is possible not to. Nevertheless, the cause and the experience of lovers happens to be just this.

Now then, one of Zeus's followers who is possessed can bear more weightily the burden of the wing-named one. Those, on the other hand, who are attendants of Ares[116] and went around with that one, whenever they are seized by Love and think they are suffering some injustice from the beloved, are murderous and ready to sacrifice both

252d themselves and the boyfriend. And thus after the manner of each god, to whose chorus each person belonged, he lives honoring and imitating that one to the extent of his power, so long as he is uncorrupted and lives out the first coming-into-being here below, and in this fashion he associates with and behaves toward beloveds and others. And so each person picks out from the beautiful ones his love after his fashion; and he constructs and adorns for himself a sort of

252e statue of that one, as a god, for him to honor and celebrate. So then, those of Zeus seek someone heavenly[117] in soul to be the one loved

113. *Kallōpizō* contains the root *kallos*, "beauty." One might translate "embellished itself." (At 236d, I have translated it "to play coy.")
114. Literally, "descendants of Homer"; admirers, reciters, or scholars of Homer are meant.
115. One is reminded of many passages, e.g., *Iliad* 1.403–4, where Homer gives names used by gods that differ from those used by men.
116. The god of war.
117. The adjective *dios* (heavenly, noble, illustrious) is closely similar to oblique cases of *Zeus*, such as *Dios* here.

by them; therefore they look into whether he is in his nature philosophic and capable of leadership, and whenever they find him and
fall in love, they do everything so that he will be such. So if they have
not previously embarked upon the practice, then they put their hand
to it and learn from wherever they can learn something, and they
themselves pursue it; and hunting to find out by themselves the na-
253a   ture of their god, they prosper through being intensely compelled to
look toward the god; and so reaching him through memory, inspired
by that one, they take up his habits and practices, to the extent that it
is possible for a human being to have a share in common with a god.
And, alleging that the beloved is the cause of these things, they cherish him still more. And if they draw the water of inspiration from
Zeus, just like bacchants pouring water onto the beloved's soul, they
253b   make him as like as possible to their god. Those, in turn, who followed after Hera,[118] seek someone kingly, and having found one, they
do all the same things regarding him. Those of Apollo, and of each of
the gods, go thus after the fashion of the god and seek the boy that is
naturally theirs; and when they have acquired him, they themselves
imitate, and they persuade and rehearse the boyfriend, so as to lead
him into the practice and *idea* of that one, to the extent of each one's
power, using neither envy nor illiberal ill will toward the boyfriend,
253c   but trying as much as possible to lead him wholly into complete likeness to themselves and the god that they honor—this is how they act.
Now then, the eagerness of those who truly love and the rite—at
least if they accomplish what they are eager to in the way I am saying—thus become, under the influence of the friend who is mad
through love, beautiful and productive of happiness for the loved
one,[119] if he is caught. And whoever is caught is indeed caught in just
such a way.

Just as in the beginning of this tale we divided each soul in three,
into some two horse-shaped forms and a third charioteer form, now
253d   too let these still stand for us. Of the horses, then, we assert that one
is good, the other not. But we did not tell fully what is the virtue of
the good one, or the badness of the bad one, but now we must say.
Well then, of the two, the one in the more beautiful position[120] is
straight in form and well jointed, somewhat hook nosed, white to the

118. Zeus's sister and wife.
119. "Loved one" here comes from the verb *philein*.
120. That is, on the right side.

sight, black eyed, a lover of honor with moderation and with a sense of shame, and a comrade of truthful opinion,[121] unbeaten, guided by command alone and speech. The other, in turn, is crooked, big and randomly slung together, strong necked, short necked, snub nosed, black skinned, gray eyed, bloodshot, a comrade of wantonness and boasting, shaggy about the ears, deaf, barely yielding to the whip and goads. So then, when the charioteer, seeing the beloved's eye,[122] heating his whole soul through with the sensation, begins to be filled with the goads of tickling and yearning, that one of the horses who is obedient to the charioteer, then as always forcibly constrained by a sense of shame, holds himself back from rushing upon the beloved. The other one no longer turns in heed either to the charioteer's goads or whip, but leaps and is carried along by force and, presenting all possible troubles to its yoke-mate and charioteer, compels them to go toward the boyfriend and to make mention[123] of the delight of sexual gratifications. These two in the beginning strive against it with irritation, on the grounds that they are being compelled to terrible and unlawful things. But at last, when there is no end to the evil, they are led to go on, giving way and agreeing to do what is bidden. And they come before him and see the boyfriend's face, flashing like lightning. And as the charioteer sees, his memory is carried toward the nature of beauty and sees it once more together with moderation, standing on a chaste pedestal. And upon seeing, he is afraid and, feeling awe, recoils on his back, and at the same time is compelled to pull the reins back so vehemently, that both horses sit down on their haunches, the one willingly through not striving against it, the wanton one very unwillingly. As the two withdraw farther off, the one soaks the whole soul with sweat from shame and amazement; the other, ceasing from the pain that it had from the bit and the fall, barely catching its breath reviles them in anger, badmouthing the charioteer and its yoke-mate in many ways, on the grounds that through cowardice and unmanliness they quit the rank and the agreement. And in compelling them against their wish to go forward again, it barely yields to their begging to put it off until later. And when the agreed-on time comes, of which the two pretend to be unmindful, by reminding, constraining,

253e

254a

254b

254c

254d

---

121. Or "truthful renown."
122. Literally, "the erotic eye."
123. More literally, "make (or compose) reminders" (*mneia*, connected with *mnēmē*, memory).

neighing, pulling, it compels them again to approach the boyfriend, for the purpose of the same speeches. And when they are nearby, it stoops down, stretches out its tail, and champs at the bit, and so pulls

254e   with shamelessness. The charioteer, however, suffering the same experience still more, recoiling as if from the starting gate,[124] drawing the bit still more with force back out of the wanton horse's teeth, bloodies the evil-speaking tongue and jaws and, causing its upper legs and haunches to rest upon the earth, gives them over to pains.[125] And when, by suffering the same thing many times, the knavish one ceases from wantonness, having been humbled at last it follows the charioteer's forethought, and whenever it sees the beautiful one, it is utterly destroyed by fear; so that then at last it happens that the lover's

255a   soul follows the boyfriend feeling a sense of shame and dread. So then, seeing that he is served with all possible service as if equal to a god, and by a lover who is not making a show of it but has truly experienced this, and that he himself is by nature friend to him who serves: even if, therefore, he has earlier been imposed upon by schoolfellows or perhaps others, saying that it is shameful to consort with a lover, and on this account he repelled the lover, now as time goes

255b   forward, maturing age and necessity lead him to admit him into his society. For at no time has it ever been allotted by fate for a bad man to be friend to a bad man nor for a good man not to be friend to a good man. When the beloved has thus admitted him and accepted both speech and association, the lover's goodwill, coming to be at close quarters, astounds him, and he perceives that all the others together, both friends and relatives, provide no allotment of friendship in comparison with the god-inspired friend. And when he continues over time to do this and consorts together, with touching, in gymna-

255c   siums and in other places of association, then at last the stream of that flow, which Zeus in love with Ganymede named longing,[126] is borne in great amount toward the lover, and part of it enters into him, and part, when he is filled to the brim, flows away outward.

---

124. That is, before the gate is thrown open to start the race (as De Vries suggests).
125. The last phrase is poetic, and reminds one of Homer, e.g., *Iliad* 5.397 and *Odyssey* 17.567.
126. *Himeros*, "longing," is again fancifully derived from the root "flow," *rheuma*; see 251c and note there. According to Homer (*Iliad* 20.232–35) Ganymede, son of king Tros (who ruled the Trojans), the most beautiful of mortal human beings, was carried off by the gods on account of his beauty to be Zeus's wine pourer. Later renditions of the tale make Zeus in love with him (see for instance Plato's *Laws* 636d). In Xenophon's *Symposium* 8.30 Socrates asserts that Zeus carried Ganymede off "for the sake not of (his) body but of (his) soul."

And just as a breeze or perhaps an echo, springing from smooth and solid objects, is borne back whence it set forth, so the flow of beauty, going back into the beautiful one through the eyes, arrives where it is naturally disposed to go into the soul and sets him on the wing; it
255d   waters the wings' passages and urges on the growing of wings and fills the beloved's soul in its turn full of love. Therefore he loves; but what? He is at a loss. He does not know what he has experienced nor can he tell; but just as someone who has caught ophthalmia from another is not able to state the cause, so it escaped his notice that he is seeing himself in the mirror, in the lover. And when that one is present, in the same ways as that one he ceases from pain; and when he is absent, again in the same ways he yearns and is yearned for, hav-
255e   ing return-love, the image of love. And he calls it, and thinks it to be, not love but friendship. In nearly the same way as that one, but less strongly, he desires to see, touch, kiss, lie down together; and then, as is likely, soon after this he does these things. So then in their lying together, the lover's licentious horse has things to say to the charioteer, and claims it deserves, in return for many toils, to have some small
256a   enjoyments. But the boyfriend's horse has nothing to say, but swelling and at a loss it embraces and kisses the lover, welcoming him kindly as being of exceeding goodwill; and when they lie down together, it is ready not utterly to deny for its own part to gratify the lover, if he should beg to succeed; but the yoke-mate, on the other hand, along with the charioteer, strives against these things, with a sense of shame and with argument. So then, if the better parts of their thought conquer, leading them into a well-arranged way of life and philosophy,
256b   they lead a blessed life and a life of one mind here below, being masters of themselves and orderly, enslaved in regard to that by which the soul's badness was arising within, freed in regard to that by which virtue was arising. And in the end, then, having become winged and light, they have won one victory in the three wrestling bouts that are truly Olympic.[127] There is no greater good than this that either human moderation or divine madness is capable of providing to a hu-
256c   man being. But if they use a way of life that is coarser and unphilosophic, but honor loving,[128] perhaps in drunkenness or in some other carelessness their two licentious yoked beasts, having caught the

127. In the Olympic Games, a wrestler had to throw his opponent three times to win and receive the victor's crown.
128. "Honor loving" (*philotimos*), like "philosophic," uses the *phil-* root for love. See second note at 256e and first note at 227c.

souls off guard and led them together for the same purpose, grasp and accomplish the choice that is deemed blessed by the many. And having accomplished this choice, now they make use of it hereafter, but rarely, seeing that they are doing things that have not been resolved by their whole thought. So then these two too, albeit less so than those for-

256d mer two, live as friends with each other, both during their love and when they have passed beyond it, in the belief that they have given and received from each other the greatest pledges of trust, which it is not righteous to dissolve so as ever to enter into enmity. And then in the end they go out of the body unwinged, yet having eagerly striven to get wings, so that they carry off no small prize of erotic madness. For it is the law that those who have once begun the journey beneath the heavens are no longer to go into darkness and the journey under earth, but

256e they are to be happy, leading a bright life, journeying with each other, and to become winged alike for love's sake, when they become so.

Such great gifts as these, boy, and divine ones, will friendship from a lover thus present you. But intimacy[129] from the nonlover, watered down with mortal moderation, administering mortal and miserly things with economy, producing in the friend's[130] soul illiberality

257a that is praised by the multitude as virtue, will make it roll mindlessly around the earth and under the earth for nine thousand years.

This palinode, the most beautiful and the best possible, within our power, has been given and paid to you, dear Love; it was compelled through Phaedrus to be stated poetically both in other respects and especially in its poetic diction.[131] Well then, with pardon for the earlier things and favor for these, kindly and propitious, may you through anger neither take away nor maim the erotic art of mine[132] that you have granted, and grant that, still more than now, it may be

257b held in honor among the beautiful ones. And if in the previous speech Phaedrus and I said anything rough[133] to you, blame Lysias,

129. *Oikeiotēs* primarily means being *oikeios*, that is, of the same family or kin.
130. The word rendered "friend's" here is the adjective *philos*, which sometimes has to be rendered "dear," as in the immediately ensuing invocation of Love (*Erōs*). The question of the relation of love and friendship (*philia*) is important, at several points in this dialogue, in the *Symposium*, in the *Laws* 8, and throughout the *Lysis*.
131. See the similar terms used in 234c by Phaedrus to praise Lysias's speech.
132. Although often denying the possession of knowledge or expertise, for instance in the *Gorgias* at 509a, Socrates on several occasions claims to have expertise concerning *erōs*: most notably in the *Symposium* at 177d–e.
133. Or "discordant," according to an alternate manuscript reading.

the father of the speech,[134] and make him desist from such speeches; turn him to philosophy, just as his brother Polemarchus has turned, so that his lover here may also no longer waver ambiguously, as now, but conduct his life simply in reference to Love with philosophic speeches.

PHAE.: I join in prayer with you, Socrates, that these things come to 257c be, if indeed these things are better for us. And I have been wondering for a long time at your speech—how much more beautiful you have made it than the earlier one. So that I shrink in hesitation, lest Lysias should appear pretty low to me, if he should then actually wish to stretch out another speech to compete with it. For indeed, wondrous man, a certain one of the statesmen[135] was lately reviling him and reproaching him for this very thing, and throughout the whole reviling he called him a speechwriter.[136] So then perhaps from a love of honor he would hold back from writing for us.

SOC.: You are stating, young man, a ridiculous opinion, and you are 257d quite missing the mark in much about your comrade, if you consider him someone thus frightened at every noise. And perhaps you actually think that the one railing at him said what he was saying in reproach.

PHAE.: He appeared so, Socrates. And you yourself know too, along with me, that those who have power to do what's greatest and are most august in the cities are ashamed to write speeches and to leave behind writings of their own, fearing the reputation in later time, lest they be called sophists.

SOC.: A sweet bend, Phaedrus, has escaped your notice—so called 257e from the great bend of the Nile.[137] And besides the bend, it has escaped your notice that those of the statesmen who intend what's greatest in their thinking most love speech writing and leaving writings behind; seeing that, whenever they write some speech, they so cherish those who approve it that they add in writing, at the first line, those who give them their approval on each occasion.

134. Compare *Symposium* 177d, where Phaedrus is called "father of the speech" and 242a–b.
135. See second note at 248d.
136. As a reproach, speechwriter (*logographos*) meant someone who made money by writing speeches for others to deliver, as the scholiast comments. Socrates, of course, takes the term in a very broad literal meaning in what follows.
137. This obscure reference to some proverb evokes, perhaps, the use of euphemism or some such trope. The explanation involving the Nile may well have intruded into the text from some grammarian's comment.

PHAE.: How do you mean this? For I do not understand.

258a   SOC.: Don't you understand that at the beginning of the political man's writing, the one who approves it has been written first?

PHAE.: How so?

SOC.: "It seemed good," I suppose he says, "to the council" or "to the people" or to both; and "so-and-so said," the writer naming himself very solemnly and extolling himself; and then he says on after this, displaying his own wisdom to those who approve, sometimes composing quite a long writing. Or does such a thing appear to you as anything other than a written speech?

258b   PHAE.: It doesn't to me, at any rate.

SOC.: So then, if this speech stays in place, the composer[138] goes away from the theater rejoicing; but if it is wiped out[139] and he gets no allotment of speech writing and of being worthy of writing it down, he himself mourns and so do his comrades.[140]

PHAE.: Very much indeed.

SOC.: It's clear, then, that they act thus not as despising[141] the practice, but admiring it wonderfully.

PHAE.: Yes, quite so.

SOC.: What then? When he becomes an adequate rhetor or king, so as,

258c   having gotten Lycurgus's or Solon's or Darius's power,[142] to become a deathless speechwriter in the city, doesn't he himself, while still living, then consider himself equal to a god, and those who come afterward believe these same things about him, when they behold his writings?

PHAE.: Very much indeed.

SOC. So then do you think that some one of such men, whoever he is and however ill minded toward Lysias, reproaches him for this very thing, that he writes?

PHAE.: It's not likely, then, from what you're saying; for it looks like he would be reproaching his own desire.

258d   SOC.: This then is altogether clear, that the writing of speeches is not, in itself, shameful.

138. *Poiētēs*: maker, poet, composer; see second note to 236d.
139. That is, from the wooden tablets on which proposed laws were written.
140. "Comrades" (*hetairoi*) can have the political connotation of fellow partisans.
141. Or "having higher thoughts than."
142. Lycurgus was the mythical lawgiver of Sparta and claimed to be guided in his legislation by Apollo (see, for instance, *Laws* 624a); Solon, one of the seven wise men, reformed Athens's laws; Darius introduced important political and financial reforms for the Persian Empire's governance.

PHAE.: No, for why should it be?

SOC.: But that thing, I think, is indeed shameful: to speak and to write not beautifully, but shamefully and badly.

PHAE.: That's clear indeed.

SOC.: What then is the manner of writing beautifully and not? Do we have some need, Phaedrus, to examine Lysias about these things, and anyone else who has ever written or will ever write, whether a political or a private written composition, in meter as a poet or without meter as a private man?

258e   PHAE.: Are you asking if we have a need? For the sake of what, then, would someone live, if I may say so, but for the sake of such pleasures? Not, I suppose, for the sake of those that one must feel pain beforehand or else not feel pleasure, which is the case for nearly all pleasures involving the body; wherefore, and justly so, they have been called slavish.

SOC. Indeed, we have leisure, as it seems. And at the same time the cicadas, singing and conversing with each other as they do in the
259a   stifling heat above our heads, seem to me to look down on us too. If, then, they should see the two of us too, just as the many, not conversing at high noon but dozing and bewitched by them through idleness of thought, they would justly laugh at us, thinking that some slaves had come to their little resting place just like little sheep to sleep at high noon by the spring. But if they see us conversing and
259b   sailing by them, as if by Sirens,[143] unbewitched, perhaps in admiration they might give the gift of honor that they have from gods to give to human beings.

PHAE.: What is this that they have? For I happen, as it seems, never to have heard of it.

SOC.: But it is surely not fitting for a man who loves music[144] not to have heard of such things. It is said that once upon a time these were human beings, before the Muses came to be; and then, when the Muses came to be and song was revealed, certain of the men of that
259c   time were so astounded by pleasure that, in singing, they lost all care for food and drink, and brought their own lives to an end without noticing it. After that the race of cicadas grew from them, having got-

---

143. These were mythical beings, half-woman and half-bird, whose beautiful singing captivated sailors and led them to crash their boats on the rocks. The most famous account of them is in Homer's *Odyssey*, book 12.

144. *Philomousos:* lover of the Muses or of music (in the broadest sense).

ten this gift of honor from the Muses, to need no nourishment when born but straightaway, without food and without drink, to sing, until they end their lives, and after that to go by the Muses and report who of those here honors which one of them. So then, by reporting

259d   to Terpsichore those who have honored her in dance troupes, they make them more favored with her friendship; and to Erato, those in erotic matters; and to the others likewise according to the form of each one's honor. To the eldest, Calliope, and to the one after her, Urania, they announce those who spend their time in philosophy and so honor the music of those two, who, most of all the Muses, are concerned with the heavens and with both divine and human speeches, and send forth the most beautiful voice.[145] So then, for the sake of many things, we must talk about something and not sleep in the high noon.

PHAE.: Yes indeed, then, we must talk.

259e   SOC.: So we must therefore examine what we just now set forward for ourselves to examine: in what way it is beautiful to speak and to write a speech, and in what way not.

PHAE.: That's clear.

SOC.: So then, for things that are going to be well and beautifully said, must not the speaker's thought already exist, with knowledge of the truth about the things that he is going to say?

PHAE.: About this matter, Socrates my friend, this is what I have

260a   heard: there is not a necessity for one who is going to be a rhetor to learn the things that are in reality just but the things that seem so to the multitude who will give judgment, nor the things that are really good or beautiful but that will seem so. For persuading comes from these, but not from the truth.

SOC.: And the word must not be thrown away, Phaedrus, that wise ones say,[146] but we must examine whether they are not saying something. And so too, what was just now said must not be dismissed.

PHAE.: What you are saying is correct.

SOC.: Should we examine it as follows?

PHAE.: How?

260b   SOC.: If I should be persuading you to acquire a horse so as to ward

---

145. The relation of the heavens, *ouranos*, to Urania is clear; Socrates also appropriates Calliope (the beautiful voiced), traditionally the Muse of epic poetry, for philosophy.
146. Partly quoting and partly adapting Nestor's words at *Iliad* 2.361: "And it will not be a word to be thrown away that I say."

off enemies, and we both should be ignorant of horses, but I should happen to know this much about you, that Phaedrus considers a horse to be that one of the tame animals that has the biggest ears—

PHAE.: It would be ridiculous, Socrates.

SOC.: Not yet. But when I should be seriously persuading you, having composed a speech of praise regarding the ass, naming it horse and saying how the creature is worth everything to have acquired both at home and on military service, useful to fight off of, and in addition able to carry equipment and beneficial in many other respects.

260c

PHAE.: Then it would be altogether ridiculous.

SOC.: So then, isn't ridiculous and friendly superior to terribly clever and hostile?[147]

PHAE.: It appears so.

SOC.: So then, when the person skilled in rhetoric, ignoring good and bad, takes on a city that is in the same condition and persuades it, not composing praise concerning the shadow of an ass as of a horse but concerning bad as if good, and having carefully studied the multitude's opinions persuades it to do bad things instead of good ones,

260d what kind of fruit do you think, after this, the rhetorical art would harvest from what it has sown?

PHAE.: Not quite a proper one, at any rate.

SOC.: Now then, good man, have we reviled the art of speeches more boorishly than need be? She might perhaps say: "What in the world, wondrous men, are you babbling about? For I do not compel anyone who ignores the truth to learn to speak; but—to give some counsel of mine—when he has acquired that, thus let him take me up. Now then, what I am saying is this big thing: that without me, he who knows the things that really are will not at all be able to persuade by art."

260e PHAE.: Will she then not be stating just things, when she says these things?

SOC.: I say yes, if, at any rate, the speeches coming at her bear witness that she is an art. For I seem to hear, as it were, certain speeches coming forward and bearing solemn witness that she lies and is not an art but an artless routine.[148] For a genuine art of speaking without grasping the truth, says the Lacedaemonian, neither is nor will ever come into being later.

---

147. "Superior" translates *kreittōn*, which I have usually rendered "stronger." See note at 238e.

148. As Socrates argues in the *Gorgias* at 463a–b and 465a.

261a PHAE.: These speeches, Socrates, are needed. Come then—lead them aside and scrutinize what they are saying and how!

SOC.: Come forward then, nobly born creatures, and persuade Phaedrus, endowed with beautiful children,[149] that if he does not adequately philosophize, he will also never be adequate at all to speak about anything. And let Phaedrus then answer!

PHAE.: Ask!

SOC.: Well then, would not the rhetorical art taken as a whole be a certain leading of the soul through speeches, not only in law courts and whatever other public gatherings, but also in private ones, the same con-
261b cerning both small and great things, and no less honored, with a view to what's correct at least, when it arises concerning serious than concerning paltry matters? Or in what way have you heard these things?

PHAE.: Not at all like this, by Zeus! But speaking and writing by art most of all, I suppose, deal with judicial judgments, and speaking also deals with speech in popular assemblies. I have not heard anything further.

SOC.: But have you then heard only of Nestor's and Odysseus's arts regarding speeches, which those two composed in writing while having leisure in Troy, but have you not heard of those of Palamedes?[150]
261c PHAE: Indeed, by Zeus, I have not even heard of Nestor's, unless you are fabricating a certain Nestor as Gorgias, or perhaps Odysseus as Thrasymachus and Theodorus.[151]

SOC.: Perhaps. But let's let these go. Now you speak: What do opposed parties in a suit do in law courts? Don't they speak in opposition? Or what shall we say?

PHAE.: This very thing.

SOC.: About the just and the unjust?

PHAE.: Yes.

SOC.: So then, does he who does this with art make the same thing appear to the same people sometimes just, and when he wishes, unjust?
261d

149. This epithet perhaps refers back to Phaedrus as the cause of many speeches (242b).
150. Homer characterizes Nestor by his age, wise counsel, and length of speech; Odysseus by his sharp intelligence and impressiveness as a speaker. Palamedes is most inventive, as De Vries puts it.
151. The long-lived Gorgias of Leontini was one of the most famous teachers of rhetoric, whose name provides the title of Plato's longest dialogue on rhetoric. Of Theodorus of Byzantium little is known beyond his having written a handbook on rhetoric, probably around 400 B.C.; Aristotle mentions him four times in the *Rhetoric*. On Thrasymachus see the note at 267d.

PHAE.: Yes; and so?

SOC.: And in speech in public assemblies, does he make the same things seem to the city sometimes good, and then in turn the opposite?

PHAE.: Just so.

SOC.: Now then, don't we know that the Eleatic Palamedes[152] speaks with art, so that to those who hear him the same things appear like and unlike, one and many, and again remaining still and carried along?

PHAE.: Very much so.

SOC.: Speaking in opposition, therefore, concerns not only law courts
261e   and speech in public assemblies but, as seems likely, there would be some one and the same art (if indeed it exists) concerned with all things said, by which someone will be able to liken everything to everything (of the things able to be likened and by those means by which it can be done)[153] and, when someone else likens and conceals it, to bring it to light.

PHAE.: Just how do you mean such a thing?

SOC.: In my opinion it will appear to those seeking in the following way. Does deception arise rather in things differing much or little?

262a   PHAE.: In things differing little.

SOC.: Well then, surely in passing over by little steps you will go toward the opposite without being noticed more than by big steps.

PHAE.: Indeed, how could that not be?

SOC.: He who is going to deceive another, and not be deceived himself, must therefore precisely distinguish the likeness and unlikeness of beings.

PHAE.: It is indeed a necessity.

SOC.: So then, will he who ignores the truth of each thing be able to distinguish the small or great likeness, of the thing that he ignores, in other things?

262b   PHAE.: Impossible.

SOC.: So therefore, for those who form opinions contrary to the beings and are deceived, it's clear that this experience slipped in through certain likenesses.

PHAE.: This is indeed how it arises.

152. Most likely Zeno, who, setting forth from the thought of Parmenides of Elea, developed famous paradoxes by which both opposites were affirmed (see for instance *Parmenides* 127e).

153. The second parenthetical clause could also mean "and for those for whom it can be done."

soc.: Is it then possible that he will be artful in causing another to pass over by small steps through likenesses, leading in each case away from the being toward the opposite (or to escape this himself), unless he has gained thorough acquaintance with what each of the beings is?

phae.: No, never.

262c soc.: Therefore, comrade, he who does not know the truth but has hunted opinions will provide for himself some ridiculous art of speeches, as seems likely, and indeed an artless one.

phae.: It may be.

soc.: Do you wish, then, to look a bit at what we assert to be artless and artful, in Lysias's speech that you're carrying and in the things we said?

phae.: Yes, most of all things, I suppose, since now at any rate we are speaking sort of nakedly, not having adequate patterns.

soc.: And indeed by some chance at least, as it seems, the two
262d speeches that have been spoken provide a certain pattern, of how someone who knows what is true would play a joke in speeches and lead the listeners astray. And I, at least, Phaedrus, hold the gods of this place to be the cause. Perhaps, too, the Muses' prophets, the singers overhead, may have inspired this gift of honor into us. For to be sure I, at least, have not any share in some art of speaking.

phae.: Let it be as you say; only make clear what you are asserting.

soc.: Come then, read me again the beginning of Lysias's speech.

262e phae.: "You know about my affairs, and you have heard what, these things having come to be, I believe to be advantageous for us. And I deem it fitting to be spared the misfortune of not getting what I ask for on this account, that I do not happen to be in love with you. For those people then repent . . ."

soc.: Stop. Now then we must say in what this errs and what it does that is artless, mustn't we?

263a phae.: Yes.

soc.: Well then, is not something of the following sort clear to everyone, that concerning some of such things we tend to be of one mind, but concerning some we are inclined to faction?

phae.: I seem to understand what you're saying, but state it still more distinctly.

soc.: When someone says the name of iron or silver, do we not all have the same thing in mind?

phae.: Yes, very much so.

soc.: What then of just or good? Are not different people carried in different directions, and do we not part ways with each other and even with ourselves?

phae.: Yes, absolutely.

263b soc.: In the ones, then, we sound in harmony; in the others, not.

phae.: That's so.

soc.: On which side, then, are we more easily deceived, and in which things does rhetoric have greater power?

phae.: It's clearly in those things in which we are wandering.

soc.: So then, he who is to go after the rhetorical art must first divide up these things in a systematic way,[154] and have grasped some characteristic of each form: that in which it's necessary that the multitude wander, and that in which not.

263c phae.: He who has grasped this, Socrates, would then at any rate have understood fully a beautiful form.

soc.: Next, I think, as he comes near each thing, he is not unaware but perceives keenly, concerning the thing that he is going to speak about, to which family it happens to belong.

phae.: Yes, and so?

soc.: What then? Should we assert that love belongs to the disputable things or to the not-disputable?

phae.: The disputable ones, doubtless. Or do you think that otherwise it would be possible for you to say what you have just now said about it, both that it is a harm to the beloved and the lover, and again that it happens to be the greatest of goods?

263d soc.: What you're saying is very good. But tell me this too—for I do not altogether remember, on account of the divine possession—whether I defined love in beginning the speech.

phae.: Yes, by Zeus, with a vehemence beyond conception!

soc.: Oh my! How much more artful do you say the nymphs, daughters of Achelous, and Pan the son of Hermes[155] are than Lysias the son of Cephalus as regards speeches! Or am I saying nothing, and did Lysias too, in beginning the erotic speech, compel us to assume Love

263e to be that certain one of the beings that he himself wished, and, having put things in order in relation to this, did he then proceed through the whole later speech? Do you wish that we read its beginning again?

154. Literally, with a road or path (*hodos*, whence *methodos* and our "method" are derived).
155. In *Cratylus* 408b–d Socrates emphasizes Pan's double nature—rough and goatlike below, smooth and human above—and his connection to speech.

PHAE.: If that seems good to you, at any rate. But what you are seeking is not there.

SOC.: Speak, so that I hear that man himself.

PHAE.: "You know about my affairs, and you have heard what, these things having come to be, I believe to be advantageous for us. And I 264a deem it fitting to be spared the misfortune of not getting what I ask for on this account, that I do not happen to be in love with you. For those people, when they have ceased from desire, repent the benefactions they have conferred."

SOC.: Surely this man, at least, seems to be far from doing what we are seeking; he endeavors to swim back again through the speech, on his back, not at all from the beginning but from the end, and begins from the things that the lover would say to the boyfriend when he has already ceased. Or have I said nothing, Phaedrus, dear head?

264b PHAE.: It is indeed, Socrates, an end, that he is making the speech about.

SOC.: And what about the other things? Doesn't he seem to have thrown the things in the speech with an indiscriminate outpouring? Or does what is said second appear to need to have been placed second out of some necessity, or any other of the things said? For it seemed to me, as to one who knows nothing, that whatever came forward to the writer was stated, not ignobly. Do you know some necessity of speech writing[156] by which that man thus set down these things in a row next to each other?

PHAE.: You are a fine one, if you consider me to be capable of thus dis-264c tinctly seeing through that man's productions.

SOC.: But I think you would assert this, at any rate: that every speech, just like an animal, must be put together to have a certain body of its own, so as to be neither headless nor footless but to have middle parts and end parts, written suitably to each other and to the whole.

PHAE.: How could one deny it?

SOC.: So then examine your comrade's speech as to whether it is in this condition or otherwise, and you will find it no different from the epigram that some say was inscribed for Midas the Phrygian.

264d PHAE.: What sort of thing is this, and what happened to it?

SOC.: This is it:

I am a bronze maiden, and I lie on Midas's tomb.
As long as water flows and great fruit trees bloom,

---

156. Or "logographic necessity."

Remaining here on this much-lamented grave,
I announce to passersby that Midas is buried here.

264e   That it makes no difference that some line of it is said first or last, you are doubtless taking note, I should think.

PHAE.: You are mocking our speech, Socrates.

SOC.: Well then, let's let this go, so that you won't be grieved—yet in my opinion it has many patterns, by looking toward which one might be benefited, by endeavoring not altogether to imitate them—and let us go on to the other speeches. For there was something in them, in my opinion, proper to see for those wishing to investigate concerning speeches.

265a   PHAE.: What sort of thing, now, are you talking about?

SOC.: The two were opposites, I suppose. For one was saying that one must gratify the lover; the other, the nonlover.

PHAE.: And very manfully, too.

SOC.: I thought you were about to say what is true: madly. This of course is the very thing that I was seeking. For we asserted that love is a certain madness. Didn't we?

PHAE.: Yes.

SOC.: And of madness, then, there are two forms: one arising from human sicknesses, the other arising from a complete change, of divine origin, away from accustomed legal usages.

265b   PHAE.: Absolutely.

SOC.: From the divine, we distinguished four parts belonging to four gods, positing prophetic inspiration belonging to Apollo, that of mystical initiation to Dionysus, poetic in turn to the Muses, and the fourth to Aphrodite and Eros; and we asserted that erotic madness is best. And in I don't know what way, we made a likeness of the erotic experience, maybe attaining some truth, and perhaps elsewhere being led astray, and so, mixing together a speech that was not alto-

265c   gether untrustworthy, we played in measured manner and in words of good omen with a certain mythical hymn and, Phaedrus, with your and my master—Eros, the overseer of beautiful boys.

PHAE.: And for me, at any rate, not at all unpleasantly to hear.

SOC.: So then, from this very place let us take up the following: how the speech was able to pass over from blaming to praising.

PHAE.: Just what, then, do you mean by this?

SOC.: The other things, it appears to me, were played with, really, in play; but these certain two forms were stated by chance, and if some-

265d one should be able to grasp their power by art, it would not be ungraceful.

PHAE.: What are they?

SOC.: For him whose sight comprehends things dispersed in many places to lead them into one *idea*, so that by defining each thing, he makes clear what, on each occasion, he wishes to teach about. Just as the things said just now about love—what it is when defined—whether they were said well or badly, the speech was able through these things to say that which is distinct, at any rate, and itself in agreement with itself.

PHAE.: And what then do you say the other form is, Socrates?

265e SOC.: To be able, contrariwise, to cut apart by forms, according to where the joints have naturally grown, and not to endeavor to shatter any part, in the manner of a bad butcher. But just as the two speeches, a little while ago, took the thought's folly as some one

266a form in common, just as from one body the parts have naturally grown double and of the same name (some called left, others right), so too the business of derangement, as the two speeches consider it one natural form in us, the one speech cut the part on the left, and cutting this further, did not leave off before it discovered among them a certain left-handed love, so named, which it reviled very much in accord with justice; the other speech, leading us toward the parts of madness on the right side, discovering something with the same name as that, a certain love that was in turn divine and,

266b holding it out before us, praised it as the cause of the greatest goods for us.

PHAE.: What you are saying is very true.

SOC.: And I myself, for one, Phaedrus, am a lover of these dividings apart and bringings together, so that I may be capable of speaking and thinking. And if I consider someone else to have the power to see the things that have naturally grown into one and toward many, I pursue this man "behind after his footstep, as if a god's."[157] Furthermore, those who are able to do this—whether I address them cor-

266c rectly or not, god knows, but however that may be, so far I call them

---

157. These words recall a half verse of Homer, "he went after the footsteps of the god" (*Odyssey* 2.406, 3.30, 5.193, 7.38; in these four passages the god referred to is a goddess—thrice Athena, once Calypso). An almost identical adverb meaning "behind" occurs with this verb for pursuing in *Iliad* 22.157, referring to Achilles' pursuit of Hector. (The Homeric passages are cited by De Vries, p. 218).

dialectical.[158] Tell us what we must call them, having learned these things now from you and Lysias.[159] Or is this that thing, the art of speeches, by using which Thrasymachus and the others have themselves become wise at speaking and make others such, whoever are willing to give them gifts, as if to kings?

PHAE.: The men are kingly, but surely not knowers of the things you are asking about. But in my opinion you call this form correctly, calling it dialectical; but the rhetorical, in my opinion, is still escaping us.

266d SOC.: What are you saying? Would there perhaps be some beautiful thing left out of these that is nonetheless grasped by art? It must not at all be dishonored by you and me; rather, what indeed it is, the remaining part of rhetoric, must be stated.

PHAE.: Very many things indeed, I suppose, Socrates, are in the books that have been written about the art of speeches.

SOC.: You reminded me beautifully, too. That a speech's preface, I think, must be said first at the beginning; these are the things you are talking about—aren't they—the subtle refinements of the art.

266e PHAE.: Yes.

SOC.: Second, then, must come some sort of narrative and testimonies for it; third, proofs; fourth, probabilities. And the man of Byzantium, the best cunning fashioner of speech, speaks, I think, of confirmation and additional confirmation.

PHAE.: Do you mean the fine Theodorus?

267a SOC.: Yes, and so? Also that one must compose refutation—yes, and sur-refutation—in accusation and in defense speech. Shall we not lead the most beautiful Evenus of Paros[160] into the middle? He first discovered allusion and incidental praise, and they say that he spoke incidental blame in meter for the sake of memory, for the man is wise. Shall we let Tisias[161] and Gorgias sleep, who say that probable things are to be valued rather than true ones, and again they make small things appear great and great things small through the might of

267b speech, and novel things in an ancient way and opposite things with

---

158. Or "skilled at dialectic." *Dialektikos* could come from *dialegō*, "to pick out" or *dialegesthai*, "to talk through" or "to converse." Perhaps some wordplay on Zeus (*Dia* in the accusative case; see 252e and note there) is suggested: dialectic as choosing Zeus—or speaking like Zeus.

159. So De Vries and Hackforth understand the sentence; some others take it to mean: "Tell us what one must call those who have learned these things now from you and Lysias."

160. He also wrote poetry and taught the young for a modest fee (*Apology* 20b).

161. A Sicilian rhetorician, one of the earliest teachers of rhetoric (especially forensic).

novelty, and they have invented conciseness of speeches and bound-less lengths concerning all things? Hearing these things from me once upon a time, Prodicus[162] laughed and asserted that he alone had discovered the art of speeches as they need to be: for they need to be neither long nor short but of due measure.

PHAE.: Most wise things, doubtless, Prodicus.

SOC.: And shall we not speak of Hippias? For I think that the for-eigner from Elis would also vote with him.[163]

PHAE.: Indeed, and why not?

SOC.: And what, again, are we to declare about Polus's musical as-

267c   pects of speeches—such as twofold speaking, speaking in maxims, speaking through likenesses—and of Licymnian names which he gave to that man[164] for the making of good diction.

PHAE.: Were not some such things, Socrates, Protagorean?[165]

SOC.: A certain correct diction, my boy, and many other things—beautiful ones too. And the Chalcedonian man's strength appears to me to have gained, by art, mastery of speeches that are dragged on, piteously wailing over old age and poverty; and at the same time the man has become terribly clever in turn at angering the many and

267d   again, when they have been angered, at beguiling them by singing incantations, as he said; and he's strongest both at slandering and at dispelling slanders from whatever source.[166] And then it looks like the end of speeches has been agreed on by all in common, to which some put the name recapitulation and others something else.

PHAE.: Are you talking about reminding the listeners, concerning the things said, of each thing in summary, at the end?

SOC.: These are the things I am talking about—and if you have any-thing else to say concerning the art of speeches. . . .

PHAE.: Small things, doubtless, and not worth saying.

---

162. The Sophist Prodicus of Ceos, whose concern with the precise use of terms is often men-tioned by Socrates, for example in the *Laches* at 197d; he is a participant in the *Protagoras*.

163. That is, with Prodicus. The Sophist Hippias of Elis claimed a wide range of expertise in various sciences; he is vividly depicted in the *Hippias Major* and *Hippias Minor*.

164. Viz. that Licymnius gave to Polus. Polus, of course, is a pupil of Gorgias best known for his role in the *Gorgias*. Aristotle mentions Licymnius as a poet as well as rhetorician in the *Rhetoric* and criticizes his making laughably excessive distinctions.

165. Protagoras, perhaps the most famous of the Sophists, has, like Gorgias and Hippias, a Platonic dialogue named after him.

166. The Chalcedonian man is Thrasymachus, already named by Phaedrus at 261c and by Socrates at 266c, and again at 269d and 271a. He appears to have been an important theo-rist of rhetoric, and he plays a major role in the *Republic*.

268a soc.: Then let's let the small things go; let us rather see these things held up to bright light—what power of art they have, and when.

PHAE.: Very forceful power too, Socrates, surely in assemblies of the multitude, at any rate.

soc.: Indeed they have. But, demonic one, you too see whether their warp appears to you also, as to me, divided.

PHAE.: Only show.

soc.: Tell me then. If someone came before your comrade Eryximachus or his father Acumenus and said, "I know how to apply to bodies certain things such as heating, if I wish, and cooling, and if it
268b seems good to me, making them vomit, and if in turn it seems good, making them excrete down below, and very many other such things. And knowing these things, I deem myself worthy to be a doctor and to make such any other man to whom I transmit the knowledge of these things."—What do you think they would say, having heard this?

PHAE.: What else, then, but to ask if they know in addition to whom they must do each of these things and when and for how long?

soc.: So if he should say, "Not at all; but I deem that, having learned
268c these things from me, he'll be worthy and able to do the things that you're asking," then?

PHAE.: I think they'd say that the human being is mad; and having heard things from a book someplace or having happened upon some little drugs, he thinks he has become a doctor, while understanding nothing of the art.

soc.: What if, in turn, someone came before Sophocles or Euripides and said that he knows how to make exceedingly long utterances about a small matter and quite small ones about a great matter, and pitiable ones whenever he wishes, and in turn the opposite, fearful
268d and threatening ones, and whatever other things of that sort, and that in teaching these things he thinks he transmits the making of tragedy?

PHAE.: These men too, I think, Socrates, would laugh at it if someone thinks tragedy is anything other than the composition of these things put together suitably to each other and to the whole.

soc.: They would not, I think, revile him boorishly, at any rate. But just as a musical person, meeting with a man who thought he was skilled in harmony on the ground that he happened to know how he
268e could make the highest-pitched and the deepest tones, would not

savagely say, "O wretch, your brain is deranged,"[167] but, since he's musical, would say more gently, "O best of men, it is necessary that one who is going to be skilled in harmony know these things too; but nothing prevents one who is in your condition from not knowing even a small bit of harmony; for you know the matters of knowledge necessary prior to harmony, but not the matters of harmonics."

PHAE.: Very correct, to be sure.

269a   SOC.: So then, Sophocles too would say the man was displaying to them things prior to tragedy but not matters of tragedy; and Acumenus would say, things prior to medicine but not medical matters.

PHAE.: Just so, absolutely.

SOC.: What then do we think honey-voiced Adrastus or likewise Pericles would say, if they heard the all-beautiful devices of art that we were going through just now—brief speech and speaking through likenesses and whatever other things we went through and said

269b   should be examined in bright light? Would they from boorishness, just as you and I, harshly say some uneducated utterance against those who wrote and taught these things as a rhetorical art, or, since they are wiser than we, would they rebuke us too, saying, "Phaedrus and Socrates, one must not display harsh anger but extend sympathetic pardon, if certain people, not knowing how to discuss, proved unable to define what in the world rhetoric is; and from this experience, having the matters of knowledge necessary prior to the art, thought they had

269c   discovered rhetoric, and, teaching others these things, they consider that rhetoric has been perfectly taught them, and that their students themselves must from themselves provide in the speeches for saying each of these things persuasively and putting the whole together, which is no great task."

PHAE.: But surely, Socrates, there is some risk, at least, that this business of the art which these men teach and write as rhetoric is something of that sort, and in my opinion what you've said is true. But

269d   how and from where might someone have the power to provide the art of what is really rhetorical and persuasive?

SOC.: Having the power, Phaedrus, so as to become a perfect competitor, is likely—and probably necessary too—to be acquired just as the other things are. If it falls to you to be by nature rhetorical, you will be a rhetor of high repute when you have acquired in addition knowledge and practice; but in whatever of these you fall short, in

167. The Greek expression means literally, "you have black bile."

this respect you will be imperfect. To the extent that an art of this exists, the approach in my opinion does not appear where Lysias and Thrasymachus proceed.

PHAE.: But where, then?

269e SOC.: It's likely, best of men, that Pericles may possibly have become the most perfect of all in rhetoric.[168]

PHAE.: Yes, and so?

SOC.: All of the arts that are great require in addition, concerning nature, babbling and talk about what's above; for this element of high-
270a mindedness and of bringing work altogether to perfection seems likely to enter in somehow from that source. And Pericles acquired this, in addition to being of a good nature. For falling in with Anaxagoras, who was such a one, and being filled with talk about what's above and attaining to the nature of mind and mindlessness,[169] concerning which Anaxagoras made his long speech, he dragged from that source toward the art of speeches what is applicable to it.

PHAE.: How do you mean this?

270b SOC.: The manner of the medical art is the same, doubtless, as that of the rhetorical.

PHAE.: How, then?

SOC.: In both one must divide up nature, that of the body in the one, of the soul in the other, if you are going, not only by routine and experience but by art, in the one case by applying drugs and nourishment to produce health and strength, and by applying with the other speeches and lawful practices to transmit whatever persuasion you wish and virtue.

PHAE.: This is likely, at any rate, Socrates.

270c SOC.: Now then, do you think one can thoroughly understand the nature of the soul, in a manner worthy of speech, without the nature of the whole?

PHAE.: If one must be persuaded in some respect by Hippocrates, of the Asclepiads,[170] it's not possible concerning the body either, without this approach.

SOC.: What he says, comrade, is indeed beautiful. But besides Hip-

---

168. The contrast with Socrates' critique of Pericles at *Gorgias* 515d–516d is striking.

169. Or "that which is not mind." Another manuscript reading conveys the pleonasm "the nature of mind and thought." See the mention of the pre-Socratic philosopher Anaxagoras at *Gorgias* 465d and the note there.

170. Doctors were frequently referred to as descendants of Asclepius, a hero mentioned in Homer's *Iliad* as having learned healing from the centaur Chiron. Hippocrates, a contemporary of Socrates, is surely the most famous doctor of Greek antiquity.

pocrates, one has to examine the argument to see if it sounds in harmony.

PHAE.: I agree.

SOC.: So then, concerning the business about nature, consider what in the world it is that Hippocrates and the true argument are saying. Must one not therefore think in the following way about the nature

270d   of anything? First, to consider whether that thing is simple or of multiple form about which we wish to be artful ourselves and to be able to make someone else artful? And next, if it is simple, to consider its power: what power does it naturally have for acting in relation to what, or what power for suffering from what? And if it has many forms, having enumerated these, to see this very same thing regarding each that one saw regarding one: by what does it naturally do what or by what does it naturally suffer what from what?

PHAE.: It may be, Socrates.

SOC.: So the approach that lacks these things, then, would be just like

270e   a blind man's way of walking. But surely he who goes after anything with art must not be likened either to a blind or to a deaf person; but it's clear that, if someone gives speeches by art to someone, he will show precisely the being of the nature of this thing to which he will apply speeches. And this, doubtless, will be soul.

PHAE.: Yes, and so?

271a   SOC.: All his struggle, therefore, has been bent toward this; for he endeavors to produce persuasion in this. Doesn't he?

PHAE.: Yes.

SOC.: It's clear, then, that Thrasymachus, and whoever else seriously gives a rhetorical art, will first with all precision write, and make us see, the soul—whether it is naturally one and homogeneous or of multiple form, in the manner of the body's shape.[171] For we assert that this is what it is to point out nature.

PHAE.: Yes indeed, by all means.

SOC.: Second, then, what it naturally does to what or naturally suffers from what.

PHAE.: Yes, and so?

271b   SOC.: And now, third, having arranged in order the classes of speeches and of soul and the things experienced by these, he will go through all the causes, fitting each together to each, and teaching through

---

171. Compare Socrates' questions about his own nature at 230a.

what cause one soul, being of such a sort, is of necessity persuaded by speeches of such a sort, and another remains unpersuaded.

PHAE.: If he were able in this way, that surely would be most beautiful, as it seems.

SOC.: No indeed then, my friend, if this or anything else is shown around or stated in some other way, it will never be said or written 271c   with art. But the people now writing arts of speeches, which you have heard, are clever rogues[172] and keep it hidden, though they know about soul in an altogether beautiful way. So then, until they speak and write in this manner, let us not be persuaded by them that they write with art.

PHAE.: What is this manner?

SOC.: To say the words themselves doesn't fall easily into place. But I am willing to say how one must write, if one is to be as artful as the situation admits.

PHAE.: Say on, then.

SOC.: Since the power of speech happens to be a leading of the soul, 271d   it is necessary that one who is going to be rhetorical know how many forms the soul has. Therefore there are so-and-so many, and of such and such a sort, from which such and such people come to be. And when these have been thus distinguished, then in turn there are so-and-so many forms of speeches, each of such a sort. Now then, people of such a sort are easily persuadable to such things by such speeches on account of this cause; people of another sort are difficult to persuade on account of these things. And then, having thought these things through competently and after that beholding them existing and being practiced in actions, one must be able to follow up 271e   on the perception quickly; otherwise, he's as yet got nothing further than when formerly he attended to hear speeches. When not only can he say competently that such a person is persuaded by such speeches but also he's able to perceive distinctly that such a one is present and 272a   point out to himself that this is the person and this is the nature that the speeches formerly dealt with, a nature that in deed is now in his presence, to which he must apply these speeches in this way for the sake of persuasion about these matters; and when, already having all these things, he grasps in addition the critical times when one must

---

172. *Panourgoi:* literally, "doers of everything," people who are ready to do anything, who stop at nothing.

speak and when one must refrain, and when, having learned what are the forms of all the speeches—of brief speaking and piteous appeal and terrible exacerbation—he recognizes the opportune time and the unfit time for these; for him, then, the art has been beautifully and perfectly accomplished, but before then, not. But when someone

272b falls short on any point whatever of these, whether he's speaking or teaching or writing, and yet asserts that he's speaking with art, he who is not persuaded prevails. "What now, then," the writer[173] will perhaps say, "Phaedrus and Socrates? Does it seem that one must accept an art of speeches spoken in this way, or in some other?"

PHAE.: It's doubtless impossible, Socrates, in any other way; and yet the work appears as no small matter, at any rate.

SOC.: What you say is true. For this reason, then, one must turn all the arguments around, up and down, inspecting them to see if some-

272c where some easier and briefer road to the art appears, so that one doesn't in vain go away on a long and rough road when it's possible to take a short and smooth one. But if somehow you have some assistance that you've heard of from Lysias or someone else, try to recall it and say.

PHAE.: As far as trying goes, I could; but right now and in this way, I cannot.

SOC.: So then, do you wish that I state a certain speech that I've heard from some of those concerned with these things?

PHAE.: Indeed—what is it?

SOC.: It is said, anyway, Phaedrus, that it's just to state even the wolf's position.

272d PHAE.: It's up to you, then. Do so.

SOC.: Well then, they say there's no need thus to make a solemn affair of these things nor to lead them up on high, bringing them round at great length. For all in all, they say—what we also said toward the beginning of this argument—that he who is going to be competently rhetorical has no need to have a share of truth about just or good deeds, or about human beings who are such by nature or by rearing. For altogether, no one has any care for truth about these things in law

272e courts, but for what is persuasive; and this is the probable, toward which he who is going to speak with art must turn. For next, one must also sometimes not say the things that were done, if they have

---

173. That is, the person who seriously gives a rhetorical art, of 271a.

not been done in a probable manner, but probable things, both in accusation and in defense speech; in all the ways one speaks, one must

273a   pursue the probable, bidding many a farewell to the true. For when this comes into being throughout the whole speech, it provides the totality of the art.

PHAE.: You have gone through the very things, Socrates, that they say who lay claim to being artful concerning speeches. For I remember that earlier we touched briefly upon such a thing as this, and this seems to be a very great matter for those concerned with these things.

SOC.: But surely Tisias himself, at least, you have studied with precision. Well then, let Tisias tell us this too: whether he says the probable

273b   is anything else than what conforms to the opinion of the multitude.[174]

PHAE.: Indeed, what else?

SOC.: Having found this, of course, a thing both wise and at the same time artful, as seems likely, he wrote that if some weak and courageous man beat up a strong and cowardly one, took away his cloak or something else, and was led into the law court, neither man of course must tell the truth. But the coward must deny that he was beaten up by the courageous man alone, and the other must contend

273c   in refutation this, that the two were alone, and must make full use of that business of "How should I, who am such as this, make an attempt on such a one as that?" And that one, of course, will not speak of his own badness, but attempting to pass off some other lie, he'd probably give over a means of refuting somehow to his adversary at justice. And about other matters, of course, some such are the things said by art. Aren't they, Phaedrus?

PHAE.: Surely.

SOC.: Whew! Tisias—or whoever else in the world, indeed, it happens to be and from wherever he rejoices at being named—is likely to have discovered a terribly cleverly concealed art. But, comrade, shall we or shall we not say to this man . . . ?

273d PHAE.: Say what sort of thing?

SOC.: This: "We happen to have been saying for a long time, before you even passed by, Tisias, that in fact this probability happens to spring up in the many through likeness with the truth; and we recently went through likenesses, saying that everywhere it is he who knows the truth that knows most beautifully how to find them. So

---

174. More literally, "what seems (sc., good or true) to the multitude."

that if you are saying something else about the art of speeches, we would listen. But if not, we will be persuaded by the things we went through just now, that unless someone both enumerates the natures
273e of those who will hear and is able to distinguish the beings by forms and to comprehend with one *idea* in accordance with each one thing, he will never be artful about speeches to the extent that this is in the power of a human being. And he will never possess these things without much diligent study. The man of sound mind must not toil away at this for the sake of speaking and acting toward human beings, but for the sake of the power on the one hand to speak things gratifying to the gods and on the other to act in a gratifying fashion in everything, to the extent of his power. For surely, therefore, Tisias,
274a wiser ones than we say that the man who has intelligence must not carefully practice to gratify his fellow slaves, except as work on the side, but to gratify masters that are good and of good ancestry.[175] So that if the road is long, do not wonder; for one must go around on it for the sake of great things, not as in your opinion. These things too, however, as the argument asserts, if one is willing, will be most beautiful when they arise from those."[176]

PHAE.: It is said altogether beautifully in my opinion, Socrates, if indeed someone might be able.

SOC.: But surely for someone who attempts beautiful things, it is
274b beautiful even to suffer whatever it befalls him to suffer.

PHAE.: Yes indeed, very much so.

SOC.: So then, let this matter about art and artlessness of speeches suffice.

PHAE.: What then?

SOC.: Then the matter about the seemliness and unseemliness of writing—coming about in what way is it in a beautiful state, and in what way unseemly—is what remains. Isn't it?

PHAE.: Yes.

SOC.: Well then, do you know in what way, concerning speeches, you will most gratify god, whether acting or speaking?

PHAE.: Not at all. Do you?

---

175. See third note at 246a.

176. "These things" refer to the less than great things with which rhetoric is concerned in Tisias's opinion; "those" designate the approaches that Socrates calls for. I take this last sentence as concluding Socrates' imaginary address to Tisias and so punctuate; some others suggest that the comment is addressed directly to Phaedrus.

274c soc.: I have something to say heard from men of former times; they themselves know the truth. And if we by ourselves should find this, would we then any longer have any care for human conjectural opinions?

PHAE.: What you asked is ridiculous. But say what you assert that you've heard.

soc.: Well now, I heard how there was, near Naucratis in Egypt, a certain one of the old gods there, whose sacred bird is the one they call Ibis. And the name of this demon is Theuth. Now, this one first

274d found number and calculation, geometry and astronomy, and further, draughts and games of dice, and then, indeed, written letters. Now furthermore, at that time the king of all Egypt was Thamos, in the upper region's great city, which the Greeks call Egyptian Thebes; and they call the god Ammon.[177] Coming to him, Theuth displayed his arts and said they must be given out to the other Egyptians. He asked what benefit each art had, and as the other went through

274e them, he expressed blame on the one hand, praise on the other, for what in his opinion the other spoke beautifully or not beautifully. Many things, then, about each art in both senses, it is said, did Thamos reveal to Theuth, to go through which would make a long speech. And when it came to written letters, "This knowledge, king," said Theuth, "will make the Egyptians wiser and provide them with better memory; for it has been found as a drug for memory and wisdom." And the other said, "Most artful Theuth, one person is able to bring forth the things of art, another to judge what allotment of harm and of benefit they have for those who are going to use them.

275a And now you, being the father of written letters, have on account of goodwill said the opposite of what they can do. For this will provide forgetfulness in the souls of those who have learned it, through neglect of memory, seeing that, through trust in writing, they recollect from outside with alien markings, not reminding themselves from inside, by themselves. You have therefore found a drug not for memory, but for reminding. You are supplying the opinion of wisdom to the students, not truth. For you'll see that, having become hearers of much without teaching, they will seem to be sensible

275b judges in much, while being for the most part senseless, and hard to

177. Several editors accept one or another emendation, which yields "they call Thamos Ammon" or "they call the god Thamos Ammon."

be with, since they've become wise in their own opinion[178] instead of wise."

PHAE.: Socrates, you easily make Egyptian speeches—and speeches from whatever country you wish.

SOC.: Well, my friend, people in the sacred temple of Zeus at Dodona asserted that the first prophetic speeches came into being from an oak tree. Now, for the men of that time, seeing that they were not wise like you young men, it sufficed, because of their simplemind-

275c   edness, to hear from an oak and a rock, if only they should say true things; for you, however, perhaps it makes a difference who the speaker is and from what country. For you do not look at only that thing: whether it is so or otherwise.

PHAE.: You have given a correct rebuke, and in my opinion the situation as regards written letters is as the Theban says.

SOC.: So then, he who supposes that he has left behind an art in writings, and he in turn who receives it with the thought that there will be something distinct and solid from writings, would be full of much simplemindedness and would fail to understand Ammon's prophecy,

275d   supposing written speeches to be something more than reminding one who knows about the things that the writings are about.

PHAE.: Most correct.

SOC.: Indeed writing, Phaedrus, doubtless has this feature that is terribly clever, and truly resembles painting.[179] For the offspring of that art stand there as living beings, but if you ask them about something, they altogether keep a solemn silence. And likewise speeches do the same. For you would think that they speak with some understanding, but if you ask something about the things said, wishing to learn, it indicates some one thing only, and always the same. And when it's been once

275e   written, every speech rolls around everywhere, alike by those who understand as in the same way by those for whom it is in no way fitting, and it does not know to whom it ought to speak and to whom not. And when it suffers offense and is reviled without justice it always needs its father's assistance. For by itself it cannot defend or assist itself.

PHAE.: These things you've said are also most correct.

276a   SOC.: What then? Do we see another speech, the brother of this one,

---

178. *Doxosophoi*, probably coined by Plato, might also mean "wise in appearance" or "wise in (others') opinion."

179. *Zōgraphia*, painting or the art of painting, has the roots "alive/animals/life" and "writing."

and genuine—do we see both in what manner it comes into being and how much better and more powerful it naturally is than this one?

PHAE.: What is this one and how do you say it comes into being?

SOC.: The one that is written with knowledge in the soul of him who understands, with power to defend itself, and knowing to speak and to keep silence toward those it ought.

PHAE.: You are speaking of the speech of him who knows, a speech living and endowed with soul, of which the written speech might justly be said to be a certain image.

276b SOC.: Just so, absolutely. Then tell me this: would a farmer who has intelligence sow seeds, if he is concerned with them and wishes them to become fruitful, in the gardens of Adonis[180] in summertime and would he rejoice seeing them become beautiful in eight days, or would he do these things for the sake of play and festivity, when indeed he would do so at all? With seeds that he is serious about, using the art of farming, having sown them where it is fitting, would he be contented when the seeds he'd sown attained their end in the eighth month?

276c PHAE.: In this way, doubtless, Socrates, he would do the one set of things seriously and the others in the other way that you're saying.

SOC.: Shall we say that he who has sciences of just and beautiful and good things has less intelligence in regard to his own seeds than the farmer?

PHAE.: Least of all shall we say this.

SOC.: He will therefore not seriously write these things in black water, sowing through a reed pen with speeches that are powerless on the one hand to assist themselves with argument, powerless on the other to teach true things competently.

PHAE.: Certainly not, as it's likely, at least.

276d SOC.: No indeed. But he will sow the gardens in writings, as is likely, and write, when he writes, for the sake of play, storing a treasure of reminders for himself, when he comes into an old age of forgetfulness; and for everyone who is going after the same track, he'll be pleased to see the gardens naturally grow up tender. But when others engage in other kinds of play, watering themselves with drinking

---

180. Special flowerpots set out to celebrate the festival of Adonis, a beautiful youth after whose premature death Zeus decreed that Adonis should spend half the year on earth with Aphrodite and half the year in the underworld with Persephone. The cult evokes thoughts of death, rebirth, and harvest.

parties and other things that are brothers to these, then that man, as is likely, will pass his time playing with the things I'm speaking of instead of these.

276e PHAE.: You are speaking of altogether beautiful play as compared with ordinary play, Socrates—of him who is able to play in speeches, telling tales about justice and the other things you are speaking of.

SOC.: So it is, indeed, Phaedrus. But much more beautiful, I think, is the seriousness that comes into being about these things, when someone using the dialectical art, taking hold of a fitting soul, plants[181] and

277a sows with knowledge speeches that are competent to assist themselves and him who planted and are not barren but have seed, whence other speeches, naturally growing in other characters, are competent to pass this on, ever deathless, and make him who has it experience as much happiness as is possible for a human being.

PHAE.: What you're saying here is indeed still more beautiful.

SOC.: Now then, Phaedrus, these things having been agreed on, we are at the point we can judge those things.

PHAE.: What sort of things?

SOC.: Things that we wanted to see about and so have come to this point here, in order that we might closely examine both the reproach

277b against Lysias concerning the writing of speeches and the speeches themselves, which might be written by art and without art. So then, what is within the realm of art, and what is not, seems to me to have been made clear in due measure.

PHAE.: It seems so, at any rate. But remind me again how.

SOC.: Until someone knows the truth of each of the things that he speaks or writes about; and becomes able to define every thing in relation to the thing itself; and having defined it, knows how, next, to cut it in accordance with forms all the way to what is uncuttable; and, seeing clearly concerning the soul's nature in accordance with these

277c same things, discovering the form that fits together with each nature, in this way sets down and orders the speech, giving speeches of many colors and embracing all harmonic modes to a many-colored soul and simple ones to a simple soul—before this he will not be able to handle with art the class of speeches, to the extent that it naturally admits of it, either for teaching something or for persuading something, as the whole earlier argument has disclosed to us.

PHAE.: Absolutely, indeed, this is doubtless how it came to light.

---

181. *Phuteuō* can mean "beget" as well as "plant."

277d   soc.: And what in turn about its being beautiful or shameful to speak and to write speeches, and in what way, when it comes to be, it might be said with justice to be a matter of reproach or not? Haven't the things said a little earlier made it clear?

PHAE.: What sort of things?

soc.: That if either Lysias or anyone else has ever written or will write, in private or in public, setting down laws, writing a political written composition, and then considering that some great solidity and clarity are in it—for someone writing in this fashion, there is matter of reproach, whether anyone says so or not.[182] For to be igno-

277e   rant, both awake and in dreams, about things just and unjust, bad and good, does not in truth escape reproach aimed at it, even if the whole mob should praise it.

PHAE.: Indeed not, then.

soc.: He, however, who considers that there is of necessity much playfulness in the written speech about each thing and that no speech has ever been written, in meter or without meter, that is worthy of great seriousness (nor spoken, in the way that recited[183] speeches are spoken, for the sake of persuasion, without examination

278a   and teaching) but that in reality the best of them are a reminding of those who know; who considers that being clear and complete and worthy of seriousness is present only in things taught and said for the sake of learning and really written in the soul, concerning things just and beautiful and good; and that he ought to declare such speeches of his to be like genuine sons, first the speech in himself, if, having been found, it is present in him, and next if some offspring

278b   and at the same time brothers of this one have naturally grown in other souls of others in accordance with their worth; and who lets the other speeches go and farewell—such a man as this, Phaedrus, is probably such as you and I might pray that I and you should become.

PHAE.: Absolutely, indeed, I for one wish and pray for the things you are saying.

soc.: So then let's consider that we have now played in measured

---

182. That is, whether or not the reproach is stated. De Vries supports a possible alternative: whether or not someone (who writes) says so (sc., that he believes solidity and clarity to inhere in his writing).

183. The verb *rhapsōdeō* refers especially to reciters of poetry. Cf. Plato's *Ion* for Socrates' examination of a famous rhapsode, and consider Xenophon's *Symposium* 3.7, where Socrates explains the view that no tribe of men is sillier than the rhapsodes by asserting that they do not understand the deeper or covert meanings.

fashion with these matters about speeches.[184] And so you go declare to Lysias that we two went down to the nymphs' stream and sanc-
278c   tuary[185] and heard speeches that enjoined us to speak to Lysias and anyone else who composes speeches, also to Homer and anyone else in turn who has composed bare poetry or poetry in song,[186] and third to Solon and whoever in political speeches has written compositions, naming them laws. If he has composed these things, knowing where the truth lies, and being able to assist, when he goes into refutative examination of the things that he has written about, and has the power, when he himself speaks, to show forth the written things as
278d   slight—such a man must not be said to be named after these things, but named after those things that he has taken seriously.

PHAE.: What names, then, do you distribute to him?

SOC.: To call him *wise*, Phaedrus, to me at least seems to be a big thing and to be fitting for god only. But either *philosopher* or some such thing would fit him better and would be more harmonious.

PHAE.: And it would be nothing beside the mark.[187]

SOC.: So then, the one who does not have things more honored than those he has composed or written, turning them up and down over
278e   time, pasting them on to each other and taking them away—will you in turn, doubtless with justice, address him as poet or writer of speeches or law writer?

PHAE.: Of course.

SOC.: Well then, declare these things to your comrade.

PHAE.: And what about you? What will you do? For one must not pass by your comrade either.

SOC.: Who is this?

PHAE.: The beautiful Isocrates. What will you report to him, Socrates? What shall we say that he is?

SOC.: Isocrates is still young, Phaedrus. But I am willing to say what
279a   I prophesy about him.

---

184. The words *pepaisthō metriōs* (". . . played in measured fashion") end Aristophanes' *Thesmophoriazusae*.

185. The word *mouseion* means "shrine of the Muses," "home of music," etc.; the same word in the plural was used at 267b in referring to Polus's work in rhetoric.

186. "Bare poetry" means without accompanying music, i.e., epic poetry; lyric poetry was accompanied with music, "in song" (*ōidei*).

187. Thus De Vries takes the sentence, comparing *Republic* 470b and *Theaetetus* 143c. Or perhaps it could mean "contrary to (his) manner." (Cf. in Thucydides 1.76, "we have done nothing contrary to the human manner.")

PHAE.: What sort of thing is it, then?

SOC.: He seems to me to be better in respect to the things of nature than the level of speeches in Lysias's circle[188] and further to have been mixed together with a more nobly born character. So that it would be nothing wondrous as his age advances if, concerning the same speeches that he now puts his hand to, he should excel by more than a man excels children those who have ever yet undertaken speeches, and still more so if these things do not suffice him but some more divine impulse should lead him toward greater things. For by nature,

279b my friend, a certain philosophy is present in the man's thought. So then these things, now, I proclaim from these gods here to Isocrates,[189] as my boyfriend; you proclaim the former things to Lysias, as yours.

PHAE.: This shall be so. But let's go, since indeed the stifling heat has become gentler.

SOC.: Is it fitting then that we proceed when we've prayed to these ones here?

PHAE.: Of course.

SOC.: Friend Pan and however many other gods are here, grant me to become beautiful in respect to the things within. And as to whatever things I have outside, grant that they be friendly to the things inside

279c me. May I believe the wise man to be rich. May I have as big a mass of gold as no one other than the moderate man of sound mind could bear or bring along.

Do we still need something else, Phaedrus? For I think I've prayed in a measured fashion.

PHAE.: And pray also for these things for me. For friends' things are in common.

SOC.: Let's go.

---

188. Following De Vries's suggestion; others take this periphrastic expression to mean simply "the level of Lysias's speeches."

189. Isocrates, a contemporary of Plato, founded a school—doubtless a rival to Plato's Academy—that taught rhetoric or, as Isocrates calls it, philosophy that guides speaking and political practice (see for example *Antidosis* 46–50). Many of Isocrates' speeches have been preserved.

The Rhetoric of Love and Learning
in Plato's *Phaedrus*

If we seek to apply Socrates' view that a speech or argument should have a unity like that of an animal, with all its parts suitably adapted to the whole, we at once confront the fact that the unity of the *Phaedrus* is not readily apparent and that various readers have taken very different views of how or even whether all the parts go together to constitute one whole. Here, I seek to develop some suggestions, broached in the general introduction, on how the several parts of the dialogue bear on the question of rhetoric.

The introductory section of the dialogue, up to where Phaedrus begins reading the speech by Lysias (at 230e), evokes many themes. Indeed, I believe that the introductions to Platonic dialogues typically do so, touching on the central theme, corollary and subordinate topics, and often other subjects and considerations that will be for the most part passed over in the dialogue but that one needs to bear in mind in order to situate the explicitly discussed issues in a more comprehensive and adequate framework. Here Phaedrus's and Socrates' exchanges mention exercise for bodily well-being, a dimension of human existence largely minimized in the subsequent account of rhetoric and love. These main themes of rhetoric and love are raised by other exchanges, which introduce the rhetorician Lysias and the speech he has written that Phaedrus characterizes as somehow erotic and reveal both Phaedrus and Socrates as lovers of speeches, to such a degree that Socrates describes himself as sick with love of speeches. Related issues foreshadowed here are the relation between the speaker's thought and the specific words that he uses, written and spoken text, the faculties of recollection and memory, and the difference between the expert and the layperson. Socrates waxes eloquent on the natural beauty of the place outside the city walls, while explaining why he nonetheless spends almost all his time with people in the city, who speak with him and can teach him something.

The longest part of the introduction raises questions about mythical stories, sophistic explanations, and Socratic investigation; it is difficult to say exactly how that section relates to all that follows. Phaedrus, having casually mentioned a mythical story about Boreas and Oreithyia, asks whether Socrates believes in such tales. Socrates notes that it would not be surprising if, like many a sophist, he did not believe them but used his cleverness to devise naturalistic explanations of them. His objection to this proceeding is that once begun, there is no end to it: additional monsters and marvels will constantly require one's attention. For Socrates, the quest to know oneself must come first; difficult to complete, it leaves him no time for inventing rationalist explanations of those myths, regarding which he remains content just to accept the conventional account. Socrates himself presents many a myth and marvelous image in his conversational investigations as Plato presents them, perhaps nowhere more than in the *Phaedrus*. In the present context, Socrates elaborates his search for self-knowledge as investigating whether he is a complex manifold wild animal like the mythical Typhon or a simpler gentler animal with some share in what is divine. That division stands in an interesting relation to Socrates' famous image of the soul in his long speech in praise of love as a god-sent madness. The soul as chariot and charioteer drawn by two very different kinds of horses is a complex or monstrous image, yet presented in a manner that explains the soul's having a share in what is divine.

Socrates' critique of sophistic explanations of myths as time-wasting rests on the boundless number of marvels and monsters, or apparently supernatural phenomena, that constantly arise. Something in human beings, it seems, forever produces such tales. Must we not have some deep-seated need for them? The important thing for Socrates is not to provide rationalist explanations of them all, but to understand ourselves. Our reasoned understanding of ourselves, as far as we can attain it, will be the standard for accepting, or rejecting, modifying, and—one suspects—making, such myths and marvels. Thus in the *Meno* Socrates tells a famous story, compatible with the *Phaedrus*'s far more elaborated images, about the soul's immortality and the consequence that knowledge is recollection of what the soul once knew. When Meno seems to accept this view, Socrates notes (and so provides us with a rare clue on interpreting his tales and images) that he would not contend for all the points of his account but would fight for the view that we would be better, more courageous, and less lazy if we believed we ought to seek for what we did not know than if we accepted the sophistic paradox that we could never find what we didn't know (86b–c). Here in the *Phaedrus*, Socrates proposes as an appropriate stance the acceptance of conventional beliefs when one has no strong grounds for rejection (as he does reject tales about battles among the gods, in the *Republic*, for instance). In harmony with this position, Socrates later criticizes Phaedrus for his sophisticated comment about how Socrates just makes up Egyptian stories as he pleases: people used to accept valuable stories from wherever they might come, Socrates says, whereas the sophisticates of the day worry about the source. Phaedrus accepts the rebuke.

After the introduction, the dialogue seems to have two main parts, one about love and the other about speeches. The most immediately visible link is that the part about love consists of rhetorical speeches (the first of which, by Lysias, is a written speech) to judge whose quality occasions the conversation about speeches (including written speeches) that constitutes the second part. Because love and rhetoric are likewise conjoined in the *Symposium*, it may help to compare these two dialogues on precisely that conjunction. The *Phaedrus* deals with rhetoric that presents love in a variety of ways, and it does so roughly half rhetorically and half dialectically. (For now I use *rhetorical*, along the lines of the very first distinction suggested by Socrates in the *Gorgias*, to mean having to do with long speeches, as compared to the give and take of dialectic, or conversational questioning and answering.) Alternatively and perhaps more precisely: rhetoric in the *Phaedrus* is first exemplified by long speeches about love and then subsequently discussed (treated dialectically). The *Symposium*, on the other hand, deals with love, but in a largely rhetorical manner, in that the treatment of love is offered largely through long epideictic or display speeches (the type of speech that Gorgias was famous for but that we miss out on at the beginning of the *Gorgias*). I say in a *largely* rhetorical manner because the simple assertion needs qualification. After Aristophanes' speech in the *Symposium*, Socrates begins a conversation with Agathon on whether one should feel shame before the few intelligent men or the many foolish ones (an issue closely linked with the difference between rhetoric for the many and discussion with the one or few that Socrates insisted on in the *Gorgias*). It is Phaedrus who interrupts those dialectical exchanges to insist on the encomia of Love that Agathon and Socrates are under an obligation to produce. And when Socrates himself delivers his own speech, he begins by establishing certain agreements in conversation with Agathon and then proceeds to report a conversation between himself and Diotima of Mantinea. Thus, in the largely rhetorical dialogue about love, the *Symposium*, Socrates nonetheless manages to speak for the most part in his usual dialectical manner. By contrast, in the *Phaedrus*'s treatment of rhetoric, Socrates makes what is perhaps his most rhetorical, his most beautiful speech of all, in praise of Love (while the dialectical exchanges deal chiefly with rhetoric).

Socrates and Phaedrus, both lovers of speeches, are brought together on this occasion by the speech of Lysias, by which Phaedrus is quite enchanted and of which he carries a copy with him. It is a seduction speech by a man seeking to win sexual gratification from a boy. To appreciate the rhetorical challenge that the speech seeks to meet, it helps to note three facts that characterized the practice of pederasty in Athens then. First, the element of erotic attraction was assumed not to be reciprocal; *erōs* did not draw the boy or youth to the older man. Second, for a beloved to gratify his lover was considered at best a somewhat dubious proposition (Lysias's speech refers to the potential beloved's, or rather nonbeloved's, desire for privacy and discretion because of the established law). Third, lovers sought boys *en hōrai*, in the bloom of youth (Lysias's speech frequently mentions the time after love has passed away along with youthful beauty); in consequence, the supply of beautiful youths is tiny in comparison with the demand.

These considerations by which pederastic love and rhetoric are interconnected are nicely stated by Pausanias in the *Symposium*. Pausanias argues that love itself and a beloved's gratification of a lover are neither simply noble nor simply base; and Athenian law reflects this ambiguity. By contrast, he says, "in Elis and Boeotia and where they are not wise at speaking, it is simply established by law that it is noble to gratify lovers, and no one whether young or old would say that it's shameful, in order, I suppose, not to have the trouble of trying to persuade the youths with speech; for they are incapable of speaking" (182b).

The distinctive and novel feature of Lysias's speech, its refined subtlety that captivates Phaedrus, consists chiefly in this, that the speaker is a nonlover who argues that the boy should gratify a nonlover rather than a lover. Now the usual approach of any lover to a beloved, in ancient Greece as elsewhere, as we may learn from much poetry or even from life, is to try to win the beloved by speaking powerfully of one's love, dilating on the depth of one's need, invoking one's passion through celebrating the beauty and other inspiring qualities belonging to the beloved. The approach taken by Lysias's speech, needless to say, stands in stark contrast with those usual amorous customs. This approach requires the display of even greater rhetorical power. Quite a tour de force is needed, and Phaedrus considers that Lysias has provided an admirable one.

Socrates responds with much playfulness and irony to Phaedrus's enthusiasm for Lysias's speech, claiming that he could provide a better one, not from himself alone but drawing on some other unnamed wise sources. Amidst the joshing, Socrates states two chief criticisms of Lysias's speech. First, though perhaps the diction may be as fine as Phaedrus believes, Socrates finds that Lysias says the same things more than once, as if ill-equipped with substantive arguments and simply showing off the capacity to say the same thing in different ways (a capacity sometimes mistaken for the whole of the rhetorical art). Second (barely alluded to here but developed in more detail in the later discussion), the ordering of the substantive matter does not impress Socrates. As he gives his own speech, Socrates presents himself as being inspired and carried away, but the most striking difference of his speech from Lysias's is its clear and logical ordering. The most interesting critique of Lysias, however, is implicit in how Socrates begins his own speech. He provides a context that is missing from Lysias's and is contradictory to its stated premise. The speech favoring the nonlover, as presented by Socrates, is said to be given by the clever lover of a beautiful boy who is loved by many. To plead his case in a distinctive manner, the lover disguises himself as a nonlover. It seems that, given the great difficulty of that task of persuasion, it would make no human sense for a nonlover to engage in it. One is left to speculate that Lysias's speech, in Socrates' judgment, was marred by deception or self-deception about *erōs* and its power. And although Socrates proceeds like Lysias to depict the lover's failings, this previously established context continues to remind us of love's great motivating power (the very aspect of love on which Phaedrus's speech in the *Symposium* focuses).

The clearly articulated order of Socrates' speech starts with a definition of love. Love of course is a desire, but everyone—lover or not—desires beautiful things. Socrates distinguishes our desire for pleasure from our acquired opinion that aims at what is best. He defines love as the desire for the pleasure of beauty when that desire without reason diverges from and prevails over the opinion that strives for what is correct. Proceeding from this definition, the speech attacks love more radically and extremely than Lysias's. The latter to be sure referred to the lover's jealousy and consequent tendency to isolate the beloved from other associations, but Socrates' speech asserts that the lover's desire to possess the beloved in unrestrained pursuit of pleasure makes him strive to render the beloved weak and dependent in all respects: ignorant and unlearned in mind, soft and delicate in bodily condition, and poor in possessions, both material and social. If Lysias's speech left one wondering why on earth a nonlover would undertake the burdensome task of persuading a much sought after lad, Socrates' leaves one wondering how a lover could possibly love what he strives so hard to debase. Lysias overturned the lover's typical attempt to make of his need a title to receive the favor of what he seeks by the lightly comic suggestion that the same reasoning would lead us to invite needy beggars rather than worthy friends to our feasts; Socrates makes of the lover's need something altogether repulsive and dangerous.

Socrates breaks off his speech at the end of the attack on love and the lover. Phaedrus, ever eager for more speech (and impressed by its quantity, for he had praised Lysias's speech for treating its topic as profusely as could be), expresses surprise and, one supposes, feels disappointment that Socrates does not state the counterbalancing praise of the nonlover. But Socrates, having already surpassed the length of Lysias's speech and professing fear of being still more excessively carried away should he continue, simply tells Phaedrus to consider the opposite things said in favor of the nonlover. We get no solid clue as to whether Phaedrus believes that Socrates' speech has surpassed Lysias's. As Socrates leads up to his second speech, which will recant the first and praise love as a divinely sent madness, Phaedrus announces that he will elicit the production of a new speech in praise of the lover from Lysias as well. After Socrates' second speech, however, which is more than three times as long as the first, Phaedrus praises it for being much more beautiful than the first and finds it so impressive as perhaps to deter Lysias from further competition. Though previously charmed by the novelty of Lysias's thesis, Phaedrus is swept along by the magnitude and beauty of Socrates' long speech, doubtless in part by its poetic character, both in other respects and especially in its diction (which Socrates attributes to the influence of Phaedrus).

Socrates praises love by first placing it among four types of divine-sent madness: prophecy, rites of purification and deliverance, inspired poetry, and love. The bulk of his speech will seek to prove that this divine madness is sent for the benefit of both lover and beloved; he announces in advance that his demonstration will be "untrustworthy for the terribly clever, but trustworthy for the wise" (245c). Thus Socrates makes the first of several distinctions among types of human beings—a capacity that he asserts later to be a crucial part of a true art of rhetoric. As he had done earlier, he here distinguishes himself (with his search for wisdom, above all for knowledge of himself) from the clever and the sophisticated. Genuine wisdom, it seems, has some connection with trust—in the present context, trust that *erōs,* that most powerful of passions, does not harmfully delude us but somehow points us toward our highest good. Along similar lines, Socrates linked distrust or disbelief with inability to remember in the *Gorgias* (at 493c), when he imagines the intemperate and insatiable man's leaky soul as unable to "hold anything on account of disbelief and forgetfulness." It is hard to spell out just how trust or belief goes along with Socratic skeptical questioning; just as similarly it is difficult to distinguish such philosophical questioning from sophistic refutation or eristic (a difficulty dramatized with comic verve in the *Euthydemus*). But the key point seems to be this: serious investigation cannot even begin without trust, as is shown by Socrates' response (involving the doctrine of recollection, mentioned previously) to Meno's sophistic objection to a proposed investigation into what virtue is. Such trust, however, cannot reasonably be fixed dogma; one must remain open to the possible need to revise the beliefs or the trust on the basis of which one began the inquiry.

After a concise argument for the immortality of soul, Socrates announces that the topic of the soul's *idea,* or what sort of thing the soul is, would require a long and divine narration. What he will give is a briefer and human account of what the soul is like, in other words, a likeness or an image of the soul. In Socrates' later discussion of rhetoric, leading the listener's soul through likenesses will emerge as the rhetor's key activity.

Socrates presents the famous image of the soul as a charioteer joined with two horses, in his endeavor to make sense of our experience of *erōs* as something noble and good. The sight of personal beauty evokes the soul's awestruck recollection of having once glimpsed beauty itself, as it followed in the train of one of the gods. The passions evoked by *erōs* are complex, in accordance with the soul's complexity—the unruly lusty horse eagerly seeks carnal satisfaction, the charioteer and the obedient noble horse experience reverence and awe. At best, *erōs* leads a lover and beloved, similar in character from having followed in the train of the same god, to lead a life of love and reciprocal friendship together distinguished by a striving to imitate the ways of their common god: philosophic like Zeus, kingly like Hera, warlike like Ares, or akin to Apollo (Socrates does not name the seven other gods). The lover is needy, as in the previous speeches; but the need highlighted here is of the noblest sort, and lover and beloved, without envy, work together to fulfill that need.

Socrates' image and account of *erōs* here stands in between his intransigently universalistic speech and Aristophanes' irreducibly particularistic speech about love in the *Symposium* in a crucial respect. Aristophanes' tale about love's origin explains love as the powerful longing to merge with the *one* other particular individual who can somehow recreate the experience of a primordial wholeness; whereas Socrates' account originating from Diotima's teaching presents love as starting from the sight of one beautiful body, moving toward bodily beauty in general, and then rising higher to other forms of beauty, ultimately to beauty itself, in an ascent that leaves all personal and particular attachments behind. Socrates' speech here repeats the linkages between *erōs* and philosophy's yearning for the vision of true reality, but like Aristophanes' it also presents the enduring attachment to a particular individual; this specific attachment is explained, however, not by an appeal to primordial individuality but by shared participation in one of eleven types of human being.

In describing how those souls that have failed to see enough of the eternal beings during a passage around heaven's vault fall to earth joined to human bodies, Socrates presents another categorization of human beings, this time into nine classes in descending order, ranked according to how much each soul has seen. No reader of Plato's *Republic* will be surprised to find the philosopher in the first rank and the tyrant in the ninth. Distinctively here, the first rank contains philosophers, lovers of the beautiful, and musical and erotic people; one could well argue that these are overlapping descriptions, or even identical at the highest level. That erotic and musical people should be in the first rank comports with *erōs*'s being a divine gift. It is surprising, given the earlier statement of three other types of divine-sent madness in addition to *erōs*, to see that those involved in prophesy and mystic rites constitute the fifth rank (after lovers of gymnastics and doctors), and poets and other imitators the sixth. The eighth rank, compatibly with Socrates' attack on sophistry and rhetoric early in the *Gorgias*, consists of the sophistic and demagogic. What Socrates attacked under the name of rhetoric as a spurious non-art of flattery in the *Gorgias* is here called demagoguery; here Socrates will be concerned more fully to elaborate what a true art of rhetoric would be, and it will prove to be inseparable from philosophy.

Because knowledge of the types of human souls will turn out to be important for a genuine art of rhetoric, one must wonder what it means to find in the same speech by Socrates one division of human soul types into nine ranks, and another into eleven classes (not to mention the three or four metallic types of the *Republic*'s best city's noble lie or the five orderings of soul elaborated later in that same dialogue). The safest conclusion, given Socrates' professions of insufficient self-knowledge, is that defini-

tive knowledge of the human soul is not available: obscurities or myster-
ies remain. Classifications—including those that an art of rhetoric will
use—must therefore be taken as tentative or provisional, subject to ongo-
ing dialectical scrutiny as well as to pragmatic testing. Certainly Socrates'
long speech about love leaves us with an immensely complex image of the
soul, monstrous in a way and yet providing an explanation for our having
a share in the divine and beautiful in its explanation of our love of the
beautiful. What moves us is complex because we are complex. The soul's
energy comes at least in part from that lusty and unruly horse. Our soul's
passionate longing points simultaneously both up and down.

Phaedrus is so struck by how much Socrates' second speech surpasses
his first in beauty that he even doubts whether Lysias would want to compete against it with a second of his own. In any case, Phaedrus comments,
one of the politicians has recently reviled Lysias as a speechwriter, and this
too might contribute to his reluctance to write again. Just as the whole
Phaedrus was occasioned by Lysias's written speech, so its second half arises
from the issue of speech writing; and indeed the dialogue's last section
will be a thematic treatment of the advantages and disadvantages of writing, culminating in a favorable reference to a better and more philosophic
writer than Lysias, Isocrates, and leaving the reader to ponder the doings
and self-understanding of the philosophic writer of this very dialogue.

After the deeply impassioned character of Socrates' long speech, the
discussions that follow seem in large measure coldly rationalistic. The investigation of rhetoric as the art of speaking well deals centrally and at
greatest length with its relation to knowledge; the discussion deals only
peripherally with passionate appeals as a part of rhetoric. Similarly, the
erotic quest, kindled by the sight of the beloved's beauty, to behold again
the true beings once glimpsed above the vault of heaven gives place to a
picture of philosophizing as gathering things together under one heading
or dividing up one being or class of beings in accordance with its natural
articulations. To the divinely mad lover of beauty and wisdom succeeds
"the man of sound mind" who toils away at these philosophic tasks not
"for the sake of speaking and acting toward human beings, but for the sake
of the power . . . to speak things gratifying to the gods . . ." (273e). Yet all
this later discussion of a different tone nonetheless takes place in the
shadow of the earlier speech. Socrates explicitly links the two by saying
that he is "a *lover* of these dividings apart and bringings together. . . . And
if I consider someone else to have the power to see the things that have naturally grown into one and toward many, I pursue this man 'behind after

his footstep, as if a god's' " (266b). The true philosophic life, indeed the highest achievement of artful speaking or writing, requires the perspectives of both halves of this dialogue. When the philosopher fails to become truly and simply wise, the philosophic life can look Sisyphean, as Leo Strauss has written: "Yet it is necessarily accompanied, sustained and elevated by *eros*. It is graced by nature's grace" (*What Is Political Philosophy?* [Glencoe, Ill.: The Free Press, 1959], p. 40).

Phaedrus the lover of speeches gladly welcomes Socrates' proposal to investigate what makes for beautiful speech writing and its opposite. Socrates encourages Phaedrus's eagerness to talk by telling the myth about the cicadas: the cicadas were men so carried away by the pleasure of newly invented music that they spent all their time singing and thus perished. Reborn as cicadas, they sing all day, without food or drink, and upon their death report humans' musical doings to the relevant goddesses. But because surely no encouragement is needed to get Phaedrus to talk and listen, the purpose of Socrates' myth must lie elsewhere. It is a cautionary tale, as Socrates suggests by comparing his and Phaedrus's conversing—instead of being bewitched into sleep by the cicadas' song—with sailing safely past the Sirens. The cicada types are not philosophers but people who love music for its own pleasure alone, without aspiration to higher insight or recollection of true being. They fall short of the most genuine human seriousness. Phaedrus runs the risk of being such a one; he is no philosopher, though perhaps he could become one. Socrates' second speech ends with a prayer that Lysias will, like his brother Polemarchus, turn to philosophy, so that then Phaedrus will no longer waver ambiguously but "conduct his life simply in reference to Love with philosophic speeches" (257b). And in the course of their discussion of rhetoric, Socrates expresses the hope that certain arguments will convince Phaedrus that, to speak adequately about anything, he must philosophize adequately (261a).

In treating rhetoric in the *Phaedrus,* Socrates takes it in a much broader sense than do the interlocutors of the *Gorgias.* In the definition he offers, it is "a certain leading of the soul" [*psychagōgia*] through speeches, in judicial and other public gatherings but also in private ones, concerning matters both great and small, serious and paltry (261a–b). Nonetheless, political rhetoric takes a place of no small importance in the *Phaedrus;* and this importance is first reflected in Socrates' objection to Phaedrus's taking the epithet *speechwriter* as pejorative. Not so, Socrates says, and he presents lawgivers as the decisive case in point. Statesmen who aim at the greatest things wish to leave behind them written speeches in the form of laws. The examples Socrates gives are surely of high stature: Lycurgus, Solon, and Darius. And Solon is named again near the dialogue's conclusion, in which Socrates proclaims that their findings about writing should be conveyed to Lysias and other composers of speeches, to Homer and other poets, and to Solon and other writers of the political speeches that are called laws.

Most of the discussion deals with beautiful and good speeches as such, whether spoken or written. Socrates' first, and abiding, point is to assert that a good speech presupposes knowledge of the truth about the subject matter of the speech in the thought of the speaker. The structure of the discussion that follows is punctuated, one might say, by Phaedrus's attempts to speak for current rhetorical teachings. Socrates shows himself to be no less informed than Phaedrus on these matters. Phaedrus interprets Socrates' Homeric-sounding allusions to rhetoricians to refer to Gorgias and Thrasymachus or Theodorus; and he later identifies one rhetorical device as coming from Protagoras. Socrates, however, mentions even more rhetoricians by name than Phaedrus and on two occasions (260d and 272d) presents arguments for current rhetorical views against his own position where one might have thought to hear from Phaedrus.

Phaedrus reports hearing that a rhetor need not learn the truth about just, good, and beautiful things; what is needed is to learn what things seem such to the multitude who will give judgment. Socrates easily makes Phaedrus see the ridiculous or harmful consequences of persuading in ignorance, but then he himself provides a rejoinder from Rhetoric herself that seems just to Phaedrus. Rhetoric does not compel anyone ignorant to study rhetoric. Let someone acquire knowledge first and then take up rhetoric; but the key point is that without rhetoric, however much else one may know, one will not be able to persuade by art. Against this conception of an art of rhetoric separate from knowledge of the truth, Socrates develops the idea that the persuasive leading of the listener's soul to wherever one wishes to lead it proceeds through likenessses. But the person best able knowingly to see and use likenesses is the person who knows the truth.

To Phaedrus's relief, Socrates turns to examples. Some things are clear and indisputable in our minds, like iron and silver; but regarding others, like the just and the good, we are carried in different ways. We are more easily led astray, and rhetoric has more power, in regard to disputable things, included among which evidently is love. Artful persuasion should begin by defining in an appropriate manner: Socrates' first speech does that, but Lysias's does not. It likewise fails to follow any necessary order in its argument and does not constitute a genuine whole. Socrates' speech (taking both as one) does provide synoptic definitions under one *idea*, and proceeds by the opposite dividing up of things according to their naturally grown joints. Socrates professes his love of these acts of dividing apart and bringing together, "so that I may be capable of speaking and thinking" (266b). He calls those capable in this regard dialectical.

Upon Socrates' asking Phaedrus whether such capacity is the art of speeches taught by Thrasymachus and others, Phaedrus replies that Socrates has described the dialectical art, but that the rhetorical art is still eluding them. In saying that, Phaedrus seems to have in mind all the devices and skills presented in books about rhetoric, of which Socrates proceeds to give many an example. Drawing comparisons to medicine, tragedy, and music, Socrates convinces Phaedrus that such pieces of knowledge are the preliminaries to or the means used by the art but not the art itself. When Phaedrus asks how someone might become really rhetorical and persuasive, Socrates answers that the acquisition of such skill depends on one's nature, acquired knowledge, and practice. Using the example of Pericles' association with Anaxagoras, Socrates suggests that the crucial knowledge acquired by Pericles, along with high-mindedness and an aspiration toward perfection, came from that source. A genuine art of rhetoric must grasp the nature of the soul, whether simple or of multiple forms; what it does and suffers; the classes of speeches and souls and the effects of each on the other. The practitioner must himself also learn to recognize the types that he faces.

That task appears long and hard. Socrates asks Phaedrus if he knows a shortcut, but Phaedrus comes up short. Socrates himself then states the view, drawn from Tisias, that all this knowledge of truth about things is not needed; what persuades is the probable. Phaedrus recognizes that to be what rhetoricians do indeed say, and remembers that he and Socrates touched on that view earlier. Socrates argues that the probable is persuasive because of its likeness to the truth; but they have already shown that the one who knows the truth is best at finding and using likenesses. The long road of diligent study must therefore be taken—not surprisingly, because it is for the sake of great things, at best, gratifying the gods. Thus the conclusion of Socrates' and Phaedrus's discussion of good speeches harks back to the gods and their connection to the highest object of our *erōs*.

Beyond knowledge of the relevant truth and the capacity to present likenesses of the truth, the art of rhetoric requires a knowledge of human souls and what speeches or arguments move each kind of soul. The effectiveness of rhetorical practice, once one assumes knowledge of the subject matter to be dealt with, would seem to increase with the degree of detail and depth of applicable insight into the soul of the addressee. Accordingly, the most fully knowledgeable and effective rhetorical practice would involve a speaker addressing one other person, about whose soul the speaker has insight sufficiently deep to enable him to address those speeches most perfectly suited to persuading that one person. This case seems to be the archetype of Socratic dialectical persuasion, whether we think of how he characterized it in his discussion with Polus in the *Gorgias*, where he rejected the calling of many witnesses and described his own procedure as calling only his single interlocutor and compelling that person to be his witness, or whether we reflect on what the philosophizing speeches between lover and beloved would be like at best, as depicted in Socrates' long speech in praise of love.

Where does this leave the possibility of artful persuasion of groups of people, for instance in political assemblies? Clearly the same full and precise knowledge and careful adaptation of speech to soul type is not possible; suitability of speeches to souls must be achieved in a rougher, approximate manner. In other words, the rhetorician could not analyze his audiences individually but would need to plan his speeches in relation to some manageable and practically relevant number of classes of soul, like the three or five of the *Republic* or the nine or eleven of Socrates' long speech. Thus public speaking—of the sort that Socrates denied engaging in in the *Gorgias*—could be knowledgeable or artful, but with a less precise and detailed knowledge than can be brought to bear on one-on-one persuasion. Socrates emphasizes the real possibility of artful rhetoric, including political rhetoric addressed to large numbers of people gathered together, by praising Pericles as perhaps the most perfect practitioner of rhetoric, in sharp contrast with his critique of him as lacking any genuine art of statesmanship or rhetoric in the *Gorgias*. The problem that a larger mixed audience poses for the practice of knowledgeable rhetoric would become most acute in the case of written speeches, because one cannot know to whom one will end up speaking and because written speeches tend to say the same thing to everyone. Also, when questioned, the written speeches cannot say something new and different to extend or defend their teaching but can only repeat the same thing.

The author's living thought must be better—more accurate or complete or comprehensive—than what he can convey in a writing (or for that matter in any particular oral speech); certainly writing it down cannot add knowledge that the writer does not already have. But writing nevertheless has great advantages—first hinted at in Socrates' insistence on hearing Phaedrus read Lysias's written speech. To elaborate the obvious: writing permits the transmission unchanged of an author's thought (or more precisely, of as much of that thought as can be expressed in writing). This advantage is perhaps most widely and strongly appreciated in the case of written laws. In Plato's own book on laws, the interlocutors take for granted that not only the laws themselves but also persuasive, educative preludes that explain the purposes of the laws will be written down. In the context of long theological arguments for the existence of gods who are concerned with human affairs, the prospective legislator Cleinias states the key advantage of writing: although the theological arguments are unfamiliar and very difficult, their being written down means that one can return to them many times to try to understand them better (*Laws* 891a).

Writings do not provide memory, they provide reminders, according to Socrates' Egyptian myth. But in the light of the other myth and image, about the soul's immortality and the related conception of knowledge as recollection, one could well think of reminders as being of high value for the pursuit of knowledge. As to their saying the same thing over and over: insofar as this is true, it is inseparable from the key advantage of writing already discussed. But surely there are ways in which this is not true. Socrates is aware of a difference between the literal or surface meaning of a text and its inner meaning. Thus, in the *Republic* he mentions hidden meanings to be found in poets' tales about the gods (378d), and in Xenophon's *Symposium* (3.7) he brings forth the idea that a thoughtful person will attain better understanding of Homer's inner meanings than the typical rhapsode possesses. Certainly most people who study a Platonic dialogue attentively find that one can in fact carry on something like a dialogue with the text: one raises objections, looks for possible answers or explanations, and may thus come to a deeper understanding of Plato's thought. A key aspect of such examination of the text is the attempt to see how it does exemplify Socrates' criteria for a good speech: that is, how is it a whole like a living being, with parts suitably fitted to each other and to the whole, arranged not at random but in an order that expresses meaning or purpose.

Writing can be taken as the most serious thing only if one forgets that the author's thought must be superior to what he can write. The charm of writing can be so great as to lead one to put it in the highest place. To be thus captivated by the charm of writing is a kind of folly comparable to the cicada types' being carried away by the pleasure of music to the exclusion of anything higher. But given that one's thinking is itself of higher rank than one's writing, the latter can nonetheless be of very high value indeed: as a reminder not only to oneself but for everyone who is going after the same track. If the writer knows more than what he has written down, so that he can assist his writings in a refutative discussion and show that his living knowledge makes his writings look slight by comparison, then—whether it is speeches or poetry or laws that he has written—he should be named for the things he takes most seriously. He would appropriately be called, Socrates says, something like a philosopher. If, however, he is most serious about his writings, which are his most honored possession, then he should be known as "poet or writer of speeches or law writer." In the *Gorgias*, Socrates suggested that poetry, stripping it of meter and music, is rhetoric. At the end of the *Symposium*, Socrates compelled Aristophanes and Agathon to agree that it belongs to the same person to write tragic and comic poetry. Here Socrates suggests that to write good speeches or arguments, good poems, and good laws may also belong to the same person, the philosopher. The best demonstration of the plausibility of that suggestion may well be the entirety of Plato's writing.